The **Rhode Island**

Family
Hiking
Guide
AND JOURNAL

Jeanine Silversmith

Maps by Julie Amy Snow

Illustrations by Mary Ercoli Walsh

42 strolls & treks for all ages throughout the Ocean State

The use of this guide is at the sole risk of the user.

Over time trails can change and signs and landmarks can be altered. If you find that conditions have changed along these hikes, please let us know so that corrections can be made in future printings. The author also welcomes other comments and suggestions. Send all correspondence to:

RI Families in Nature
PO Box 5211
Wakefield, RI 02880
info@rifamiliesinnature.org

Silversmith, Jeanine
        The Rhode Island Family Hiking Guide and Journal—42 strolls & treks for all ages throughout the Ocean State.

Library of Congress Control Number 2015943208
ISBN 978-0-692-46351-2

Published by RI Families in Nature
PO Box 5211
Wakefield, RI 02880
www.rifamiliesinnature.org

Maps by Julie Amy Snow
Illustrations by Mary Ercoli Walsh
Cover and book design by Maureen Sternin
Back cover photo by Adam Sternin

For Sierra and Devin, my favorite hiking buddies.
Your little legs have taught me great things.

Acknowledgements

This book would have remained just an idea were it not for the many people who helped make it happen.

Thank you to Julie Amy Snow, Mary Ercoli Walsh, and Maureen Sternin for taking on the pieces that had me paralyzed with fear and to Sheryl Kaskowitz for her thoughtful and thorough editing.

Thank you to the organizations and agencies dedicated to managing the natural spaces in Rhode Island and to their staff members who work tirelessly to protect spaces for hiking and help people enjoy them.

For believing I could join their ranks well before I did, I would like to thank authors Cliff Vanover, Leah DeCesare, Anna Solomon, Christine Carr, and Marybeth Reilly McGreen.

I would also like to thank my many wonderful friends for testing out these hikes, giving me excellent advice, and offering their unwavering support, especially Sue McCue, Mara Ostro, Elisabeth Bux, Elisa Lucia, Sarah Bell, and Anisa Raoof.

Thank you to my family, who cheerfully (for the most part) accepts my crazy tree-hugging ways. Specifically I want to thank my mother and father, Ann and John Posa, for having the brilliance to tell me to "go outside and play" virtually each and every day of my childhood.

Above all, I want to thank my husband, Ian, for his constant support and encouragement. Thank you for being my partner in love and life.

Contents

Introduction

When I first became a parent, finding the time and motivation to hit the trails with my children was very difficult. I have always loved hiking, but I wasn't sure where to go or how to do it with little legs following me. My idea of an "easy" hike didn't seem so easy when my kids were with me. Three miles was no longer a "short" distance, but a potential eternity. You see, my children are not particularly strong or even intrinsically motivated to hike. They are ordinary kids who sometimes (okay, often) get tired, cranky, and belligerent, just like every other kid. But I have always recognized how much better my children behaved, ate, and slept if we ran around, climbed some trees, and splashed in puddles.

So, I started to search out family-friendly hikes: those that offer easy access, clear trail signs, interesting features, and ample opportunity to bail out and head home. Soon, my quest for family-friendly hikes morphed into a futile quest for a Rhode Island family hiking guide. And so this book was born.

Since I moved to Rhode Island in 2004, I've been amazed by the number and quality of state and town parks, nature preserves, wildlife refuges, and management areas. Over 20 percent of the Ocean State's nearly 700,000 acres are protected. Consisting of only 1,200 square miles, with its highest point (Jerimoth Hill, hike #20) only 812 feet above sea level, Rhode Island is full of relatively short, manageable hikes that aren't too far from home. So while Rhode Island may be the smallest state in the U.S., it's certainly big on natural places for families to explore. Each year, my family and I continue to find new gems that we add to our long list of favorites.

Hiking is an excellent way to slow down, spend more time with our families, enjoy and explore natural places, and reconnect with each other. Our lives have become more complicated and overscheduled with the demands of school, work, and home—not to mention the increasing amount of time spent in front of computers, televisions, and mobile devices.

You most likely know the health benefits of walking. As heart disease, obesity, and diabetes rates reach epidemic proportions, incorporating exercise into our lives has become nothing less than essential. Hiking not only provides the opportunity for physical activity, but also for interaction with the natural world—something that happens far too infrequently in our society, given all of the benefits it offers (see *The Benefits of Being in Nature*, page 3).

This guide includes 42 of my family's favorite hikes for people of all ages and abilities. I've included short, stroller- and wheelchair-accessible walks as well as long, rugged treks, and a whole lot in between. Just as families and family members differ in their abilities and interests, each hike in this book has its own characteristics and features. Some include walking along the beautiful shoreline or to lakes, ponds, and rivers; other hikes offer a spectacular view of Providence or the Blackstone Valley; still others offer a chance to observe local wildlife or evidence of glaciers that covered Rhode Island long ago. Along with essential and helpful information for each hike, I've included a section for you to record your observations and experiences, and make personal notes for future visits.

I hope this book encourages you to carve out time to explore the Ocean State's natural places, to enhance your family's health and well-being and, just as importantly, to help you connect with each other and have fun. See you outside!

The Benefits of Being in Nature

Just like healthy food and a good night's sleep, spending time in nature is beneficial. For me, being outside simply feels good and seems to have a pretty remarkable effect on my outlook and mood. But you might be surprised, as I was, to learn just how essential time in nature is to our health and well-being and how extensive the effects are.

There is a growing body of research showing the connection between unstructured play and interaction with the natural world and the physical, mental, and emotional health of both children and adults. Research studies show that children who regularly spend time outside are healthier, happier, and smarter than those who do not.

According to scientific studies, people who regularly spend time in nature experience the following effects:

• ***They are healthier.*** Not only does the risk of obesity decrease, but vitamin D production, gross-motor development, and sleep are all positively affected by time in nature. Plus, there are fewer cases of myopia (near-sightedness) in people who spend significant periods of time outside.

• ***They do better in school.***
Children who regularly spend time in nature have higher grades and fewer symptoms of Attention Deficit and Hyperactivity Disorder than those who do not. Preschoolers who spend

time outside have increased literacy skills, and people of all ages can experience a concentration boost after spending time outside.

- **They feel better about themselves.** Not only do they have better self-esteem, confidence, and self-discipline when they spend time outside, but people learn to cope with everyday pressures and manage risk better!

- **They are good problem-solvers.** Perhaps it's the ever-changing landscape or the open-ended challenges, but spending time in nature can improve problem solving and critical thinking skills.

- **They are more creative.** Life is full of distractions, stimuli, and pressures: think cell phones ringing, traffic jams, work deadlines, and the latest news report. Taking time away gives our bodies and minds a break from these stressors and a chance to be productive in a completely different way.

- **They are more cooperative.** Studies show that simply being surrounded by the natural world can lead to a decrease in crime and aggressive behavior, strengthen relationships between neighbors, and help build strong communities.

- **They feel connected with nature and are tomorrow's conservation leaders.** It might be obvious, but those of us who have plentiful and varied interactions with nature are more likely to fully appreciate it. In addition, a commitment to protecting the environment stems from firsthand experiences with it.

As you can see, there are many reasons to get outside and hike with your family. And here's one more: it's also a ton of fun!

For details on the scientific research supporting these positive effects of spending time in nature, see the *Appendix* on page 201.

How to Use This Book

This book features 42 hikes throughout Rhode Island, categorized by how challenging they are for children. Strolls are typically short, flat, and easy. They are great for young or inexperienced hikers, or when you can only squeeze in a short outing. Some are even stroller-friendly and wheelchair-accessible. Treks, on the other hand, are longer and generally more difficult to navigate. There might be a steep incline, or the trail might be rockier and require more attention. Treks are best suited for older kids or more experienced hikers.

The Choice Is Yours
How to choose a hike

When choosing a hike, take everyone's ages, physical abilities, and interests into consideration. You know your family best. Keep in mind that some 4-year-olds can hike for a long time while some 12-year-olds are not at all motivated or physically capable. If you are new to hiking as a family, start with strolls and work your way up. That being said, if your family is comfortable taking on longer, more rugged hikes, don't disregard strolls, which can offer wonderful experiences for seasoned hikers. Similarly, don't be afraid to try out a trek just because you're inexperienced or your family includes a young hiker. You can always turn around early or just hike one section.

To choose a hike, you can simply browse the pages and see what strikes you as appropriate and interesting, or this book offers a few helpful tools to get you started. Whichever method you use, involve your children in the process so that they're motivated from the beginning. The ultimate goal is to simply get outside and have fun. This may require you to adjust your expectations—something I will readily admit was difficult for me at the beginning. Remember: it's all about the kids!

Looking for a spot nearby or in a particular town? Check out the *Map of Hikes* on page 26. Keep passing signs for a park and want to learn more? Check out the alphabetical *List of Hikes* on page 27. Notice that the number associated with each hike relates to its position on the map.

Need a bit more information or don't know where to start? Check out the *Hike Chart* on pages 28-31. Not only is the distance and relative difficulty of each hike listed on the chart, but it also includes important information such as whether or not dogs are allowed, if the path is stroller- and wheelchair-accessible, and if hunting is permitted. In addition, the chart highlights interesting features of each hike, such as waterfalls, playgrounds, and observational platforms, which are particularly helpful in getting children excited about an outing. In my experience, I've found that asking if anyone wants to "go look for toads" or "check out a waterfall" elicits far more enthusiasm than simply announcing "Let's go on a hike!" In fact, I am sometimes greeted by howls of "Nooooooo!" when I say this—and I'm the one who wrote a family hiking guide! So whether you want to enjoy a refreshing swim after your hike, need to find a hike easily accessible by public transportation, or you're potty-training your toddler and want to make sure there are bathrooms onsite, this chart lays it all out for you. All of the information on the chart corresponds to the icons that are included in each hike's description. You will also find a column to keep track of which hikes you have completed.

And again, whichever hike you choose, just remember the ultimate goal: getting outside and having fun.

Let the Book Be Your Guide

Once you choose a hike—but before you head out the door—read through the description with your family to help you prepare for and enjoy your hike.

The icons, which correspond to the information that is listed in the *Hike Chart* on pages 28-31, are as follows:

	stroll (hike that is typically short, flat, and easy)
	trek (hike that is longer and generally more difficult)
	my favorite season(s) to visit (spring, summer, fall, winter)
	bathrooms or porta-potties
	stroller- and wheelchair-accessible
	visitor or nature center
	picnic tables
	leashed dogs allowed (always leash, curb, and clean up after your dog)
	hunting permitted
	swimming
	public transportation (within 1.5 miles)
	fee

The *Overview* is a short paragraph that points out the features and highlights of the hike. This section can help you decide which hike to choose and get your children excited to visit the property.

The following information is included in the *Logistics* section for each hike:

- the length of the hike
- the address
- the GPS coordinates
- directions to the hike (usually from the nearest highway or major road)
- property website (Since details are subject to change, be sure to call or check a property's website before you head out.)

Some hikes require special equipment or are at least better enjoyed if you bring along something in particular. Equipment that is specific to each hike is listed under the *What to Bring* section. (For a list of basic equipment to bring on each outing, see page 13.)

Next, you will find a paragraph with information about what to look for *On the Trail*. I've included details such as which trail to take, features to look for, tips on how to navigate the trail safely and any precautions to take, whether or not there is an opportunity to extend the hike, and more.

And finally, each hike has its own *Trail Map* that is conveniently labeled with the number and name of the hike. There is also a legend on each map.

Blaze a Trail
How to use this book while you are hiking

While hiking, refer often to the hike's *Trail Map* and *On the Trail* section. Try to involve your kids when you do. Ask them if they want to see where you are on the map. Explain what's up ahead on the trail. This will encourage them to be observant and attentive hikers.

You might find that during some of your hikes, your kids are excited, interested, and motivated and there is no lack of things to talk about and explore. Other times, for whatever reason, you might find that your children—as mine often do—need a distraction from simply walking in the woods. Be creative! Use games, songs, and whatever else you have in your magic parenting hat to keep your kids from getting bored or tired. For a list of tips and tricks, see *Happy Trails* on page 17.

Taking Time to Reflect
How—and why—to use the journal pages

After each description, you will find a few pages for your family to use for reflection during and after the hike. I cannot emphasize enough how enriching this activity can be for your family—especially your children! When kids take some time to record their thoughts and observations, they are given a chance to interpret their experiences, as well as develop awareness of their relationship with the natural world. In our fast-paced, screen-filled world, it's wonderfully refreshing and healthy to sit for a few minutes (or more) in the fresh air with nothing but a blank page, a pencil, and our thoughts.

Some kids love drawing pictures; others love using a camera. Some kids like creating poems; others like recording the weather and the wildlife and plants they noticed. Keeping this in mind, I've included questions and prompts on the left

side of the journal pages and an open space on the right side where kids can draw, attach photos, and write creatively.

From a purely logistical standpoint, it's also nice to keep notes on where you have gone hiking to refer back to when you want to return. My family records a whole slew of information, such as which friends we should tell about the hike, what we should bring next time, where we parked—even what restaurant we went to afterwards and how good the pancakes were.

You're a Winner!
Claim your reward

Getting exercise and exploring nature with your family offers many rewards (see *The Benefits of Being in Nature*, page 3). Furthermore, if you hike all 42 strolls and treks in this guide, I feel your family deserves a prize!

Here's what you do:

• Have your children record their thoughts and observations in the journal section following each hike description. If your child is too young or uninterested, feel free to take on this job until they are willing and able to do so.

• Use the prize as motivation to hit the trails! It's a fun challenge. However, be sure to set a realistic time frame for your family to complete all 42 hikes. This will likely take a year or two.

• Contact me at info@rifamiliesinnature.org to receive your prize.

• Don't worry! Your copy of *The Rhode Island Family Hiking Guide and Journal* is yours to keep.

Guidelines and Suggestions for a Successful Hike

Any outdoor activity involves some risks, even if we do not act wildly or irresponsibly. So there are a few things to keep in mind before, during, and after you hit the trails that will help you plan and successfully carry out appropriate hikes. Furthermore, it's nothing less than a recipe for disaster to set adult goals and expectations for kids while you're hiking. With this in mind, I've shared everything I have learned (mostly the hard way) about getting out the door and enjoying an outing.

Prep Time
Before the hike, take ample time to plan and prepare your family for your adventure. This list of what to do to plan and prepare might seem overwhelming at first, but I can assure you that the more you hike, the easier it will be to get out the door. As the saying goes, today's actions become tomorrow's habits.

• **Consider the distance, difficulty, and features** of a hike to be sure it is appropriate and exciting for each person in your family. Involve your children in the process of selecting a hike (see page 5 for help in choosing a hike).

• **Call or look online** to check directions, fees, hours, and other details that are subject to change.

• **Let someone know where you're going** and when you expect to return.

- **Teach yourself and your family how to prevent tick bites.** Protect yourself from ticks by wearing the most effective repellents: Clothing that's been treated with the repellent Permethrin is the best deterrent; repellents containing DEET that are applied to exposed skin are far less effective against ticks. Wear long, light-colored pants tucked into

long, white socks. Learn more at the website for the University of Rhode Island's TickEncounter Resource Center (www.tickencounter .org).

- **"Leaves of three, let it be. Hairy vine, no friend of mine."** Make certain everyone in your group can identify poison ivy.

- **Eat a satisfying and nutritious meal** before heading out to prevent fatigue and irritability.

- **Check the weather.**

- **Dress appropriately.** Wear hiking boots or sturdy sneakers, and dress in layers of weather-appropriate clothing. For the colder months, invest in some absorbent synthetics, fleece, and waterproof jackets if you can, and don't forget hats and gloves. For hotter weather, try to steer clear of heavy cottons that can hold perspiration and remember sun block, sunglasses, and sun hats.

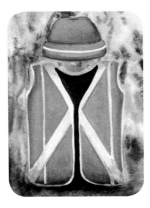

- **In some areas, all users, including hikers, are required to wear 200 square inches of solid daylight fluorescent orange** (either a hat or a vest) during the hunting season. This is usually—but not always—from the second Saturday in September to the last day of February, and from the third Saturday in April to the last day in May, annually. Hikers are required to wear 500 square inches (a hat AND a vest) during shotgun season, which is usually from early December through early January. For information about this year's hunting season and regulations, visit the Rhode Island Department of Environmental Management's website at www.dem.ri.gov.

- **Pack emergency supplies,** including:
    - a well-stocked first aid kit
    - prescription medications
    - a watch to keep track of the time
    - a whistle for each member of your party (they can be heard farther away than a person's voice, and take less energy to use)
    - a cell phone, turned off or silenced
    - a flashlight, in case the sun sets before you return to your vehicle
    - a compass
    - matches
    - a pocketknife

- **Include these other essential and/or helpful items** in your back-pack:
    - extra clothes and socks, including rain gear
    - sunblock
    - bug repellent
    - plenty of high energy snacks (see *Happy Trails #5*, page 18)
    - water in fun, reusable bottles
    - *The Rhode Island Family Hiking Guide and Journal*
    - writing implements (unlike crayons and markers, colored pencils don't melt or dry out!)
    - magnifying glasses
    - binoculars
    - camera
    - field guides
    - infant carrier
    - diapers, wet wipes, small changing mat, and waste bags
    - items for your dog such as a leash, treats, water bowl, and waste bags

• **As soon as your children are able to carry a backpack, let them!** They can carry their own water and snacks, or *The Rhode Island Family Hiking Guide and Journal* and writing implements. Encourage them to decide which items they would like to carry and expect some redistribution along the trail as they get tired or simply interested in something you're carrying. If your child is adamantly opposed to carrying a backpack, don't fight it too hard. They'll come around sooner or later.

On the Trail

During the hike, keep everyone safe, motivated, and content along the way.

• **Set behavioral expectations before you start.** In parenting as well as in my career as an educator, I've found that kids are much more likely to follow rules that they've had a hand in setting. So before you tell them the "dos and don'ts" of hiking, ask your children for their ideas.

• **"Stay on the path, stay with the group, and if you're lost, hug a tree."** This is my golden rule of hiking, which we repeat at the start of each and every outing. By hiking in the middle of the path, you are less likely to get lost, damage plants, cause erosion, run into poison ivy, or pick up ticks. Although your group may have to spread out a bit on the trail, everyone should be able to see each other along the way. Stop when the trail curves and at trail intersections. If you do get separated or lost, staying in one spot helps searchers find you far more quickly, and you won't be injured in a fall or in another type of accident. Hugging a tree or another stationary object and even talking to it or singing a song helps keep you calm—and then you get to call yourself a tree hugger!

- **Confirm your position** by regularly checking your map and using the trail markers, if available. Most trails are marked with paint blazes or small signs/markers on trees, rocks, and posts. A good rule of thumb is to look for your next trail marker as soon as you pass one. When you cannot see a trail marker, stop and look in all directions before proceeding. Sometimes you may have  to look behind you to make sure you're still on the trail. If you come upon two markers on one tree, the top marker indicates which direction to turn—right or left.

- **Take frequent breaks.** Young or inexperienced hikers tire easily; be prepared to turn around sooner rather than later, even if this means not "finishing" your hike.

- **Children, especially very young ones, might impress you with how much fuel they need on a hike.** Offer snacks and water regularly and as motivation to get to that next bench, tree, or other milestone.

- **Keep an eye on the weather;** it can change quickly.

- **Stay mindful of ticks, sun exposure, and poison ivy.** Reapply bug spray and sunblock as needed.

- **One of the most appealing aspects of hiking is the chance of a wildlife sighting.** How thrilling! While it's perfectly fine to get a closer look at small and harmless creatures (insects, spiders, toads, etc.), never approach or try to touch larger or more dangerous animals. If you find yourself too close for comfort with an animal, stay calm, avert eye contact, slowly back away, and do not run.

- **Praise and encourage your child.** Use games, songs, and activities to keep your kids from getting bored or tired. Your kids (and you) will stay interested and motivated if they don't perceive the hike as a forced march through the woods (see *Happy Trails*, page 17).

- **Record your observations and experiences** in *The Rhode Island Family Hiking Guide and Journal*.

In summary, hike smart and have fun!

After the Hike
The Four Rs: Remove, Refuel, Reflect, and Rest

Replenish your bodies and spirits sooner rather than later.

- **Do a tick check** immediately upon completing the hike, and again when you return home. Visit www.tickencounter.org for more information on how to remove ticks safely. If you find a tick, be sure to take a picture and try to identify it. TickEncounter's TickSpotters program will help confirm the tick identification and provide guidance for managing the tick bite and preventing future bites.

- **Refuel** with a healthy, hearty meal and plenty of water.

- **Talk with your kids about the hike** and be sure to highlight the positive aspects. Ask them what they'd like to do for your next hike. You may want to add more observations and notes in the journal pages.

- **Don't be surprised how tired children can be after a hike.** Be on the lookout for signs of fatigue and (bonus!) put them to bed early.

Happy Trails: Tips for Family Hiking

Along with the guidelines and suggestions on pages 11-16, here are a few other tips and tricks to keep your family happy, interested, and motivated while you're hiking.

Back to Basics
General Ideas

1. **Remind each other of the golden rule.** "Stay on the path, stay with the group, and if you're lost, hug a tree." (See page 14 for an explanation.)

2. **Learn the hiker's creed.** "Take only pictures. Leave only footprints. Kill only time." Please do not collect anything from wildlife refuges, nature preserves, and other areas that prohibit the collection of natural objects. Pack out all of your trash. And teach your children to respect nature enough not to destroy or damage plants, animals, or anything else you encounter on the trail.

3. **Be here now.** Some kids, especially very young ones, will stop every few feet to examine seemingly mundane objects. If you allow children to explore at their own pace, you will likely find that the depth of the experience completely outweighs the distance you have covered. And for the love of Pete, please turn off your cell phone and make a commitment to use it only in the case of an emergency. Teach your

children that time in nature is important and enjoyable enough not to be interrupted by phone calls, text messages, and emails.

4. **Praise and encourage your child.** A compliment from a loved and trusted adult means so much to a child. Tell them how much you enjoy spending time with them outside, how proud you are of them for behaving appropriately in nature, how impressed you are with how far they've hiked—just as you encourage them to read or praise them for eating their vegetables. Spending time outside is just as vital to their health and happiness and should also be fostered as a lifetime habit.

5. **Become a GORP connoisseur.** GORP ("good old raisins and peanuts") has come to mean just about any trail-friendly snack of mixed yummies. Come up with your own family GORP recipe using dried fruit, nuts, sunflower or pumpkin seeds, shredded coconut, soy nuts, pretzels, Goldfish®, Cheerios®, candies such as M&Ms® or Reese's Pieces®, or anything else your kids really love, perhaps something they don't eat often. Avoid anything that will easily melt or freeze.

6. **Use peer pressure to your advantage.** Invite friends and other families along on an outing and you just might be surprised at how much faster and/or farther your kids hike. Consider joining RI Families in Nature (www.rifamiliesinnature.org) and attend our monthly hikes.

7. **Tempt them with a payoff.** Instead of saying, "Let's go hiking," use an enticement such as "Let's go look for seals!" (John H. Chafee Nature Preserve, hike #21) or "I know where we can climb to see a beautiful view of Providence" (Neutaconkanut Hill, hike #28).

8. **Motivate the curmudgeon.** Sometimes there is one family member who is not very interested in the prospect of walking in the woods. Put him in front and let him be the leader. Or ask him to try the hike

for 15 minutes and then let him decide if he wants to turn back. (Hey, 30 minutes on the trail is better than none!)

9. **Reward your children.** Whether it's a small physical item such as a compass or field guide, an experience such as going to the library, or even a delicious treat, don't be afraid to reward your children for hiking. Make your long-term goal to complete all 42 strolls and treks in this book, and tell your kids you'll receive a prize for doing so (see page 10).

10. **Mix it up.** Ask your children to hike with you on your birthday or incorporate a hike into your holiday activities. Try out a new hike next time you find yourself in a part of the state you don't get to that often. Do whatever it takes to make hiking a regular part of your life.

11. **Don't be afraid of rain—or snow for that matter.** Kids of all ages love jumping in puddles and crunching snow under their feet. Grab the raincoats and rain boots, or snow pants and snow boots, and make the best of a seemingly crummy situation. Just remember to never play outside when there's thunder and lightning.

12. **Relax, laugh, and have fun!** Demonstrate your own enthusiasm (or fake it a little) and your children might enjoy hiking more than you thought they would.

Child's Play
20 fun activities to try on the trail

It's always helpful to have something up your sleeve when you find that your child is bored, tired, or acting unsafely or inappropriately while you're hiking. Although some of these ideas may seem best suited for very young children, you might be surprised how easily your older children will engage in these simple games and activities.

1. **Count.** Whether it's birds, flowers, clouds, or trail markers, counting anything in nature will help little ones feel motivated to go forward.

2. **Gather.** Collect leaves, shells, rocks, or acorns—and then remember to return them before you go. Keep an eye out for the gift of walking sticks! Each hiker tries to find "just the right stick" to hike with and then sets them against a tree or informational kiosk at the end of the hike for others to find and enjoy.

3. **I Spy.** This old favorite is a guessing game in which one player chooses an object that is visible to all, and gives a clue such as the object's color or initial letter by saying, "I spy with my little eye something (red, beginning with the letter s, etc.)." The other players have to guess what the object is.

4. **Play the alphabet game.** Find something on the trail that starts with the letter a, then b, and so on. We get creative with this one and use words like "quiet" and "exercise."

5. **Poetry in motion.** Work as a team to make up silly poems or stories. One person starts with a line or sentence, with each person taking turns to add a line or two.

6. **Identify stuff.** Some children really want to know the official name for things they find on the trail. Pretty much the only field guides we use in our family are the *Peterson's First Guides* and the laminated *Pocket Naturalists* series. They contain the most common species and are much more manageable in the woods than the thicker, more thorough guides.

7. **Listen up.** This is a good one for when you're taking a break. Everyone sits comfortably on a bench, log, or on the ground, closes their eyes, and listens for different sounds. Every time you hear a sound, raise a finger. Then, tell each other the sounds you heard. Expect accurate as well as imaginative recollections!

8. **Sing a song.** Softly sing your favorite tune or make up words about the hike to fit into a familiar melody.

9. **Pretend.** Imagine you are living in the forest long, long ago and pretend to hunt or gather food.

10. **Be a shutter bug.** Take turns using a camera to document the trip.

11. **Take a closer look.** Bring along either magnifying glasses or binoculars (or both) and expand your hiking experience.

12. **Ask a question.** This is one of my favorites. In the age of busy schedules and extensive screen time, it seems we're losing the inclination and ability to engage in conversation. Take advantage of this time with your family to ask simple, open ended questions to your young children or to dive into deeper topics with your tweens and teens.

13. **Go on a scavenger hunt.** Go to www.rifamiliesinnature.org/hiking-scavenger-hunt/ and print out a copy of our scavenger hunt. Feel free to modify according to your liking and/or location and season. Don't forget the clipboards and pencils!

14. **Go treasure hunting.** If you have a GPS device or GPS capability on your cell phone, check out geocaching at www.geocaching.com. If you're without GPS, look into letterboxing at www.letterboxing.org, in which players use clues and navigational skills to find hidden treasures. Many of these treasures are hidden on the properties in this guide.

15. **Bark like a tree.** Hold a piece of paper firmly against the trunk of a tree. Peel a crayon and rub it sideways on the paper until you get an impression of the bark. Collect several tree rubbings and compare the patterns.

16. **Play 20 questions.** In case you don't remember the rules or never learned them, here's a refresher: One person chooses a common object (not a proper noun or a specific person, place, or thing). Everyone else takes turns asking yes or no questions to try to figure out what it is. The trick is to try to guess within 20 questions.

17. **Solve a mystery.** One person explains a scenario with a very limited and somewhat vague set of clues (and knows the solution) and everyone else tries to solve it by asking yes or no questions. For mysteries and solutions, check out your local bookstore—I'm partial to the *One-Minute Mysteries and Brain Teasers* series—or do a web search for "minute mysteries" or "lateral thinking puzzles."

18. **Pay the toll.** My own children developed this game on a hike when they were particularly bored . . . I mean, creative. They take turns holding a small branch or stick in front of the rest of the family to prevent them from walking along the trail and then ask us to "pay the toll" by finding a rock, acorn, something that starts with a certain letter, etc. When each of us presents or points out the object, we are allowed to pass and continue the hike.

19. **Let them go.** Their games may seem silly, even strange, at times, but remember you are encouraging them to develop creativity, social skills, and a sense of awareness. The author Richard Louv speaks of "constructively bored kids"—kids who, when allowed a bit of time to be in the here and now, eventually create a game to play, develop an art project to work on, or find some interesting leaves to collect. Keep them safe of course, but let them go.

20. **Learn more.** In *Hikes with Tykes: Games and Activities*, author and hiker Rob Bignell has put together an extensive list of more than 100 activities, crafts, recipes, games, and post-hike activities for every age group and interest.

Join In
Organizations and Events

1. **Participate in the Great Outdoors Pursuit.** Organized by the Department of Environmental Management, the Rhode Island Great Outdoors Pursuit helps you and your family enjoy recreational resources and outdoor activities throughout the state while learning and engaging in healthy lifestyle choices. Each pursuit features free and low-cost activities such as hiking, fishing, kayaking, rock climbing, and children's games, as well as music, food, environmental and health-related exhibits, raffles, and give-aways. Learn more at www.riparks.com/RIOutdoorsPursuit.

2. **Join a club.** There are many wonderful organizations that can help your family get outside through guided walks, book recommendations, information about their properties, and more. Here are a few with chapters in Rhode Island:
   - Appalachian Mountain Club, Narragansett Chapter: www.amcnarragansett.org
   - Audubon Society of Rhode Island: www.asri.org
   - The Nature Conservancy of Rhode Island: www.nature.org/rhodeisland
   - RI Families in Nature: www.rifamiliesinnature.org
   - Rhode Island Land Trust Council: www.rilandtrusts.org
   - Rhode Island Sierra Club: www.rhodeisland.sierraclub.org

3. **Volunteer.** Many nature groups organize service days that include trail clearing, bench building, tree planting, and other down and dirty activities that will engage and educate children. There are sometimes age minimum requirements, so be sure to check before you go.

4. **Attend an outdoor community event.** Check your local print or online news sources to find out what's going on in or around your

town. Check out KidoInfo at www.kidoinfo.com, a fantastic resource for finding family-friendly natural places to explore, outdoor events, and a whole lot more.

Et cetera
A few other resources

1. **Read a book by Richard Louv.** If you want to learn more about the research findings that support the notion that time outside is healthy for you and your children, check out *Last Child in the Woods* or *The Nature Principle*.

2. **Support the movement.** The Children & Nature Network (www. childrenandnature.org) is an international organization that works to connect children, families, and communities with nature through part-nerships, resources and tools, and support of grassroots efforts.

3. **Join the conversation.** The Providence Children's Museum created PlayWatch, a listserv dedicated to connecting the community around the greater topic of children's play. Members can share ideas, infor-mation, resources, articles, events and more. Join at www.children museum.org/PlayWatch.asp.

4. **Support environmental education.** The Rhode Island Environmental Education Association promotes formal and informal environmental education. Go to www.rieea.org to learn more.

Map of Hikes

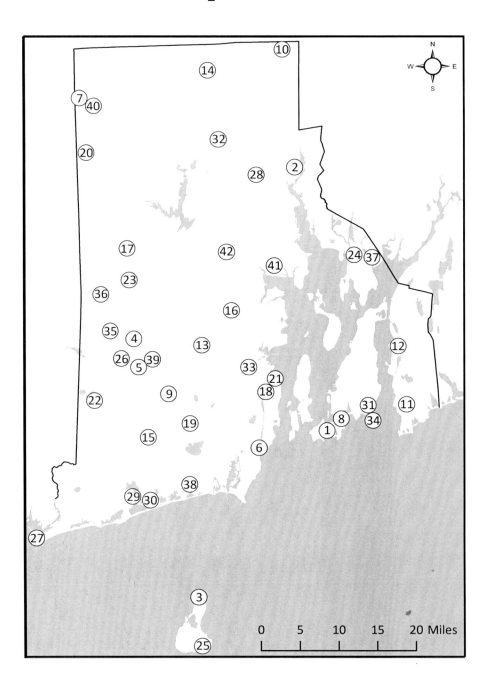

List of Hikes

Hike Chart

#	Pg	Name	Town	Stroll or Trek	Dist	Ext (mi)	When to Visit	Facilities	Strollers
1	32	Ballard Park	Newport	👣	1.1		☀	🚻*	
2	36	Blackstone Park	Providence	👣	1.0	var	🌱		
3	40	Block Island Nat. Wildlife Refuge	New Shoreham (Block Island)	👣	1.5		☀ ☘	🚻*	
4	44	Breakheart Pond Loop	Exeter	👣	1.5	2.0	🌱		
5	48	Browning Mill Pond	Hopkinton	👣	1.5		☀ ☘		
6	52	Canonchet Farm	Narragansett	👣	1.5	3.0	☘ ❄	🚻*	
7	56	Casimir Pulaski Memorial State Park	Chepachet	👣	1.3	10.0	☀ ❄	🚻*	
8	60	Cliff Walk	Newport	👣	1.2	7.0	🌱 ☘	🚻*	🛒
9	64	Crawley Preserve	Richmond	👣👣	2.0	3.0	🌱 ☀		
10	68	Diamond Hill Park	Cumberland	👣👣	1.5		🌱 ☘		
11	72	Dundery Brook Trail	Little Compton	👣	1.2	2.2	🌱 ☀	🚻*	🛒
12	76	Emilie Ruecker Wildlife Refuge	Tiverton	👣	1.5		☘		
13	80	Fisherville Brook Wildlife Refuge	Exeter	👣	1.3	2.75	☀ ☘	🚻	
14	84	Fort Nature Refuge	North Smithfield	👣	1.5	3.8	❄		
15	88	Francis C. Carter Memorial Preserve	Charlestown	👣	1.0	1.9	🌱		
16	92	Frenchtown Park	East Greenwich	👣👣	1.2	2.1	🌱 ☘		
17	96	George B. Parker Woodland	Coventry	👣👣	2.0	4.5	☀		
18	100	Gilbert Stuart Birthplace & Museum	Saunderstown	👣	1.0		🌱	🚻	
19	104	Great Swamp Management Area	West Kingston	👣👣	4.0	6.2	🌱 ☘		
20	108	Jerimoth Hill	Foster	👣	0.5		🌱 ☘		
21	112	John H. Chafee Nature Preserve	North Kingstown	👣👣	2.7		❄		

Hike Chart

Vis Ctr	Picnic Tables	Dogs	Hunting	Swimming	Pub Trans (mi)	Fee	Features	✓
		🐕			🚌 1.0		scenic views, vernal pond, meadow, old quarry	
		🐕			🚌 0.3		river, ponds, playground, giant staircase	
🏠*							beach, ocean views, birds, lighthouse (fee)	
		🐕	🎣				scenic views, waterfalls, streams, bridges	
	⛱	🐕	🎣				scenic views, stone walls and pavilion, fish hatchery	
		🐕		🏊	🚌 0.2	$* pkg	scenic views, boulder, S. County Museum (fee)	
	⛱	🐕	🎣	🏊			beaver dam, beach	
		🐕			🚌 0.7	$* pkg	ocean views, Forty Steps, Newport mansions	
		🐕	🎣				rocky, rugged paths	
	⛱	🐕					scenic views, old ski footings, band shell	
	⛱						pond, swamp, boardwalk, playground	
							scenic views, observation blind	
							pond, cemetery, bird boxes, meadow	
							ponds, beaver dam, deciduous and evergreen forests	
		🐕	🎣				meadows, bird boxes, vernal pools	
		🐕					pond, Tillinghast Mill ruins	
							cairns, signage, meadows, brook, structure	
🏠*	⛱				🚌 1.2	$	scenic views, cemeteries, tours (included in fee)	
		🐕	🎣		🚌 1.3		migratory birds, wetlands, monuments	
		🐕	🎣				highest point in the state	
		🐕			🚌 0.2		harbor seal viewing, scenic views, Rome Point	✓

seasonal

Hike Chart

#	Pg	Name	Town	Stroll or Trek	Dist	Ext (mi)	When to Visit	Facilities	Strollers
22	116	Long Pond Woods	Hopkinton	👣👣	2.2		☀		
23	120	Maxwell Mays Wildlife Refuge	Coventry	👣	1.3	3.0	🌱		
24	124	McIntosh Wildlife Refuge	Bristol	👣	1.0		❄	🍴	🛒
25	128	Mohegan Bluffs	New Shoreham (Block Island)	👣👣	4.0		🌱 ☀	🍴	
26	132	Mount Tom	Exeter	👣👣	1.5	4.0	☘		
27	136	Napatree Point Conservation Area	Westerly	👣	2.0	3.0	☀	🍴	
28	140	Neutaconkanut Hill	Providence	👣👣	1.5	2.0	☘		
29	144	Ninigret Nat. Wildlife Refuge (northern)	Charlestown	👣	0.8	1.75	🌱	🍴	🛒
30	148	Ninigret Nat. Wildlife Refuge (southern)	Charlestown	👣	1.3	4.2	🌱 ☘	🍴	🛒
31	152	Norman Bird Sanctuary	Middletown	👣👣	3.5	var	☀	🍴	
32	156	Powder Mill Ledges Wildlife Refuge	Smithfield	👣	0.9	2.75	🌱	🍴	
33	160	Ryan Park	North Kingstown	👣	1.0		☘		
34	164	Sachuest Point Nat. Wildlife Refuge	Middletown	👣	1.2	2.5	☀ ❄	🍴	🛒
35	168	Stepstone Falls	Exeter	👣	3.0		🌱		
36	172	Tillinghast Pond Management Area	West Greenwich	👣👣	2.2	4.0	☀		
37	176	Touisset Marsh Wildlife Refuge	Warren	👣	1.1		🌱		
38	180	Trustom Pond Nat. Wildlife Refuge	South Kingstown	👣	1.8	2.5	☘	🍴	
39	184	Upper Roaring Brook	Hopkinton	👣	0.5	var	❄		🛒
40	188	Walkabout Trail	Glocester	👣👣	2.0	8.0	☀	🍴	
41	192	Warwick City Park	Warwick	👣	2.8		🌱 ☘	🍴*	🛒
42	196	West Warwick Riverwalk	West Warwick	👣	1.0		❄		🛒

Hike Chart

Vis Ctr	Picnic Tables	Dogs	Hunt-ing	Swim-ming	Pub Trans (mi)	Fee	Features	✓
							scenic views, hemlock forest, ponds	
							pond, cemetery, meadow	
🏠					🚌 0.1		scenic views, boardwalk, Environmental Educ Ctr. (fee)	
🏠*		🐕		🏊			beach, lighthouse, ocean views, petting zoo	
		🐕	🎯				scenic views, rock ledges	
		🐕*		🏊			beach, ocean views, Fort Mansfield carousel (fee)	
		🐕			🚌 0.1		scenic views, monument, playground, skate park	
🏠	⛱	🐕					Kettle Pond Vis. Ctr., ocean views, spotting scope	
🏠				🏊			fishing, canoeing/kayaking, playground, airfield	
🏠	⛱					$	scenic views	
🏠					🚌 0.1		pond, stream, rock walls, ASRI Headquarters	
	⛱	🐕	🎯				scenic views, fishing, canoeing/kayaking	
🏠	⛱						ocean views, observation platforms, spotting scopes	✓
		🐕	🎯				waterfall, old pavilion	
		🐕	🎯				scenic views, boulders, fishing, canoeing/kayaking	
							marsh, river, meadows	
🏠							salt pond, observational platforms, spotting scopes	
		🐕	🎯				boardwalk, pond, stream	
	⛱	🐕	🎯	🏊		$*	beach, boulders	
	⛱	🐕		🏊	🚌 0.6		beach, paved path, athletic fields, playground, dog park	
		🐕			🚌 0.1		river views, waterfall	

seasonal

Overview

Newport's only nature preserve seems much larger than its 13 acres, partly because it is adjacent to a wildlife refuge and partly due to the grandeur of the views and rock features. There are gorgeous vistas, a vernal pond, lush woodlands and swamps, diverse wildlife and plant species, interesting rock outcroppings, and a large puddingstone boulder left by glaciers over 10,000 years ago. Granite was quarried here from the early 1800s to the 1930s, and you can see evidence of this throughout the park and in the Quarry Meadow, a great spot for a picnic as well as the site of many public events.

Logistics

- 1.1 mile
- corner of Hazard and Wickham Roads, Newport
- 41.468007,-71.322945
- Directions: From America's Cup Avenue, follow Thames Street south all the way; it will turn into Carroll Avenue. At the fork, bear right onto Old Fort Road. At the stop sign take a right onto Wickham Road. Proceed up the hill; Ballard Park is on the left. Parking is available across the street at Rogers High School or on Hazard Road.
- www.ballardpark.org

What to Bring

- basic equipment (see page 13)
- rock & mineral field guide
- bug spray
- picnic

On the Trail

My favorite thing about Ballard Park is that it's small enough to let my kids just wander about, choosing the trails they want to follow. They feel like real explorers and I know we're never really that far from the car. That being said, the trails here are unmarked, so it's important to refer to the map often as you hike. A nice route to follow begins at the

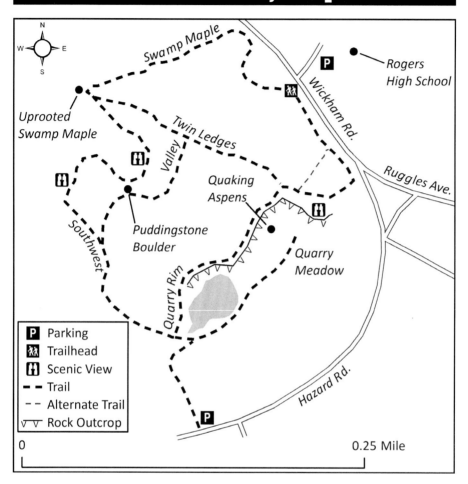

- **P** Parking
- 🚶 Trailhead
- 🚻 Scenic View
- •• Trail
- -- Alternate Trail
- ⌄⌄ Rock Outcrop

0   0.25 Mile

Wickham Road entrance across from Rogers High School. Go right on the Swamp Maple Trail and follow to a swamp maple tree, uprooted by a storm years ago. Turn right to go up a short but steep incline onto the Southwest Trail to the Joseph Cotton Overlook. Take special care here, as the drop off is quite steep and dangerous. Continue past the puddingstone boulder and around to the Quarry Meadow. Take some time to explore, rest, and refuel, then head back along the Quarry Rim Trail. Take a right onto the Twin Ledges Trail for a view of the meadow from above, again taking extra care along the edge. Follow the Swamp Maple Trail back to the Wickham Road entrance.

Date _____ Time _____ to _____

Weather: ☀ ⛅ ☁ 🌧 ❄ 🌬

We hiked with _____

On our hike, we saw _____

We found _____

We heard _____

We smelled _____ We felt _____

Our favorite part of the hike was _____

Our least favorite part was _____

For this hike, it was important to bring _____

What surprised us about this hike was _____

One word to describe this hike is _____

Restaurants or attractions nearby: _____

_____

We would / would not do this hike again because _____

_____

We would tell our friends that this hike _____

_____

Use the space below to draw a picture, attach a photo,
or write more about your hike.

#2 Blackstone Park, Providence

Overview
Blackstone Park and the 1.6-mile Blackstone Boulevard greenway are maintained by the Blackstone Parks Conservancy in partnership with the Providence Parks Department and the Department of Public Works. The 45-acre park contains easy trails and many features that children will love to explore. This is a very popular spot for locals to walk their dogs (often unleashed), so try to go in the middle of the day and be aware of your surroundings. Besides the lush woodlands, ponds, and views of the Seekonk River, there is a giant staircase, conservation areas, and a playground. It's hard to believe you're within a half mile of bustling Wayland Square!

Logistics
- 1.0 mile; you can extend your hike on various side trails
- corner of Rhode Island Avenue and Paterson Street, Providence
- 41.830569, -71.382180
- Directions: From Route 195 East, take exit 2 for India Street toward Gano Street. Keep left at the fork, then turn left onto India Street. Turn right onto Gano Street, travel 0.7 mile, and turn right onto Waterman Street. Make the second left onto Butler Avenue. Then, turn right onto Rhode Island Avenue. The intersection with Paterson Street is in about 0.1 mile. The trail is just south of the playground on Paterson Street.
- www.blackstoneparksconservancy.org

What to Bring
- basic equipment (see page 13)
- long pants to protect against poison ivy

On the Trail
Although the trails are not marked in Blackstone Park, you're always somewhere between and usually within view of the Seekonk River and a Providence roadway. The trail starts next to the playground on Paterson Street in the southern section of the park. In about 100 feet, turn left and walk along the ridge. Notice Blackstone Pond below you and the Seekonk River beyond that. Following along this trail, you'll soon reach Angell Street. Cross carefully and follow the path into the middle section of the park. Here the paths are wide and flat and lined with logs to keep you

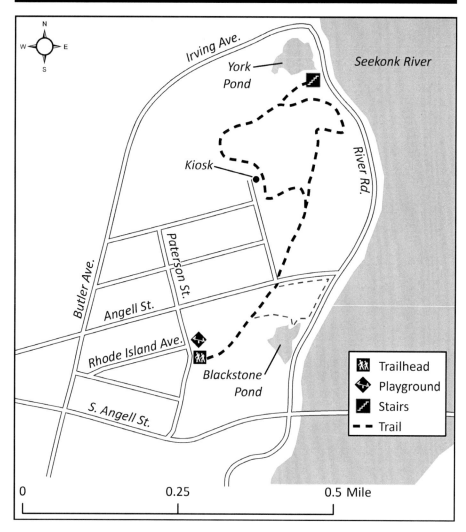

from wandering off the trail and causing soil erosion (a problem the Conservancy has been working hard to mitigate). Follow the path through the middle section until it turns right toward the river. Take the outer loop closest to the river until you reach the top of a large staircase that leads down to a ravine. This is a neat place to explore and take a rest, but you'll have to climb back up the stairs to continue around the outer loop. Turn right and continue straight until you reach a kiosk along Parkside Road. Head back into the woods and turn right to retrace your steps to the playground.

Date _____ Time _____ to _____

Weather: ☀ ⛅ ☁ 🌧 🌨 🌬

We hiked with _____

On our hike, we saw _____

We found _____

We heard _____

We smelled _____ We felt _____

Our favorite part of the hike was _____

Our least favorite part was _____

For this hike, it was important to bring _____

What surprised us about this hike was _____

One word to describe this hike is _____

Restaurants or attractions nearby: _____

_____

We would / would not do this hike again because _____

_____

We would tell our friends that this hike _____

_____

Use the space below to draw a picture, attach a photo,
or write more about your hike.

Overview

At the northern tip of Block Island, at the very end of Corn Neck Road, is a 133-acre bird watcher's paradise. In the fall, Block Island National Wildlife Refuge (NWR) is a stopover point on the Atlantic Coast for dozens of species of birds, some rare or endangered. Even if you're not a birder, this walk along the beach and a visit to the North Lighthouse & Interpretive Center are well worth your time. While the refuge is open year round for hiking, be certain to call the town of New Shoreham to check on lighthouse hours and admission fees.

Logistics

- 1.5 miles
- Corn Neck Road, New Shoreham (Block Island)
- 41.224699,-71.567437
- Directions: A car, bicycle, or taxi is recommended to reach the entrance, since it is over 4 miles from the ferry landing. From the Old Harbor ferry landing, take a right onto Water Street, which turns into Dodge Street. Take your first right onto Corn Neck Road and follow all the way to the end for the entrance to the Block Island NWR.
- www.fws.gov

What to Bring

- basic equipment (see page 13)
- sand- and water-friendly shoes or sandals
- binoculars
- bird guide
- admission fee for the North Lighthouse & Interpretive Center

On the Trail

From the entrance, walk along the beach until you see a path fork off to the left. Follow this to the North Lighthouse. The narrow path behind the lighthouse will loop around to the very tip of the island and bring you back along the northern shoreline.

40

#3 Block Island National Wildlife Refuge, New Shoreham

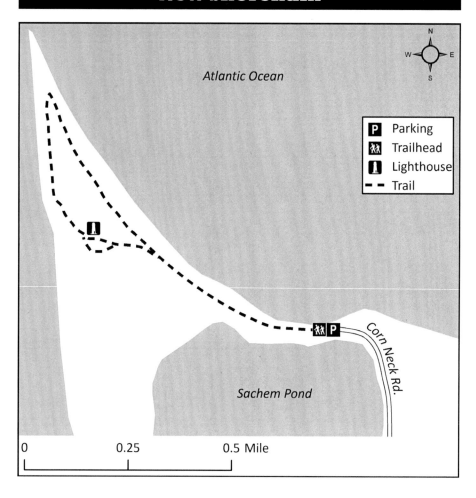

Atlantic Ocean

N
W — E
S

P	Parking
🚶	Trailhead
🗼	Lighthouse
- -	Trail

🗼

🚶 P

Corn Neck Rd.

Sachem Pond

0   0.25   0.5 Mile

#3 Block Island National Wildlife Refuge, New Shoreham JOURNAL

Date _____ Time _____ to _____

Weather: ☀ ⛅ ☁ 🌦 🌨 🌬

We hiked with _____

On our hike, we saw _____

We found _____

We heard _____

We smelled _____ We felt _____

Our favorite part of the hike was _____

Our least favorite part was _____

For this hike, it was important to bring _____

What surprised us about this hike was _____

One word to describe this hike is _____

Restaurants or attractions nearby: _____

_____

We would / would not do this hike again because _____

_____

We would tell our friends that this hike _____

_____

42

#3 Block Island National Wildlife Refuge, New Shoreham JOURNAL

Use the space below to draw a picture, attach a photo,
or write more about your hike.

Overview
With over 14,000 acres, Arcadia Management Area is Rhode Island's largest recreational area, and offers many opportunities for outdoor activities such as hiking, mountain biking, boating, fishing, and horseback riding. This book includes five of the many, many trails in Arcadia. The first is the loop around Breakheart Pond, an easy trail to follow with many wonderful views of the 44-acre pond. Swimming is not allowed in Breakheart Pond, but fishing and boating are.

Logistics
- 1.5 miles; 2.0 miles or more if you extend along intersecting trails
- off Frosty Hollow Road, Exeter
- 41.596317,-71.703969
- Directions: From Route 3 South, make a right onto Route 165. Travel for 2.8 miles and make a right at the West Exeter Baptist Church onto Frosty Hollow Road. Travel 1.5 miles, past the Frosty Hollow trailhead. Make a right and follow to the very end to the parking lot at the pond.
- www.riparks.com

What to Bring
- basic equipment (see page 13)
- binoculars for the view across the pond
- solid daylight fluorescent orange during the hunting season

On the Trail
At the northern end of the parking lot, you'll find the beginning of the Breakheart Pond Loop Trail. After a short while, you'll walk over several bridges across streams and small waterfalls. Keep the pond to your right at all intersections, as this trail hooks up with several others. Of course, you can extend your hike by taking any of these intersecting trails. Just be sure to bring along a map of the surrounding area (found on the Department of Environmental Management website, www.dem.ri.gov/maps).

#4 Breakheart Pond Loop, Exeter

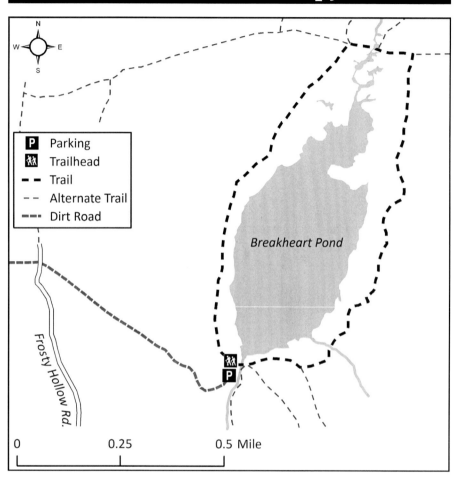

P Parking
Trailhead
- - Trail
- - Alternate Trail
- - Dirt Road

Breakheart Pond

Frosty Hollow Rd.

0   0.25   0.5 Mile

Date _____ Time _____ to _____

Weather: ☼ ⛅ ☁ 🌧 🌨 🌬

We hiked with_____

On our hike, we saw _____

We found_____

We heard_____

We smelled _____ We felt _____

Our favorite part of the hike was _____

Our least favorite part was_____

For this hike, it was important to bring _____

What surprised us about this hike was _____

One word to describe this hike is _____

Restaurants or attractions nearby: _____

_____

We would / would not do this hike again because _____

_____

We would tell our friends that this hike _____

_____

Use the space below to draw a picture, attach a photo,
or write more about your hike.

Overview

At first glance, this might seem like just another loop trail around a pond in Arcadia Management Area. But Browning Mill Pond has unique features that make it truly different from Breakheart Pond and worth a separate trip. With a large picnic area, old stone walls and pavilion, a dam, an old fish hatchery, and a lovely pond, it's easy to see why Browning Mill Pond is one of the more popular spots in Arcadia.

Logistics

- 1.5 miles
- Tefft Hill Trail and Arcadia Road, Hopkinton
- 41.555870, -71.685065
- Directions: From Route 3 South, make a right onto Route 165. Travel for 1.4 miles and make a left onto Arcadia Road. The parking area is about 1.4 miles down, the first right after the Pavilion sign on your right and the Browning Mill Pond Recreation Area sign on your left.
- www.riparks.com

What to Bring

- basic equipment (see page 13)
- picnic lunch
- Frisbee or ball for catch
- solid daylight fluorescent orange during the hunting season

On the Trail

From the parking lot, pick up the yellow-blazed loop trail and go clockwise around Browning Mill Pond. In a short while, you'll come to a wooden fence. To your left are the rectangular, man-made ponds that were once part of a fish hatchery. On the second part of the trail, you'll cross several footbridges and see the remnants of a rather large stone pavilion. Keep the pond to your right to follow the trail back

48

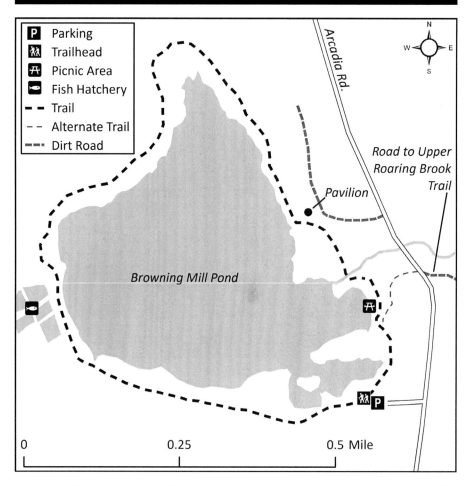

Legend:
- **P** Parking
- Trailhead
- Picnic Area
- Fish Hatchery
- – – Trail
- – – Alternate Trail
- –··– Dirt Road

Arcadia Rd.

Road to Upper Roaring Brook Trail

Pavilion

Browning Mill Pond

0   0.25   0.5 Mile

towards the parking lot. Just before you return to your vehicle, you'll reach the large picnic area with a beautiful view of the pond. You can also combine this hike with the Upper Roaring Brook Trail (hike #39) across the street.

#5 Browning Mill Pond, Hopkinton JOURNAL

Date _____ Time _____ to _____

Weather: ☼ ⛅ ☁ 🌧 🌨 🌬

We hiked with _____

On our hike, we saw _____

We found _____

We heard _____

We smelled _____ We felt _____

Our favorite part of the hike was _____

Our least favorite part was _____

For this hike, it was important to bring _____

What surprised us about this hike was _____

One word to describe this hike is _____

Restaurants or attractions nearby: _____

_____

We would / would not do this hike again because _____

_____

We would tell our friends that this hike _____

_____

Use the space below to draw a picture, attach a photo, or write more about your hike.

Overview
Narragansett's beaches are known throughout and beyond Rhode Island, but there are lots of other wonderful natural places to explore. For example, within the 174 acres of Canonchet Farm, there are both salt- and fresh-water marshes, an old quarry, Pettaquamscutt Cove, as well as a rich cultural and natural history featured in the South County Museum. In addition, the trail system is well maintained, and the Friends of Canonchet Farm are happy to answer questions and help you out. Parking is available on Anne Hoxsie Lane and at the Narragansett Town Beach lots; parking fees apply from Memorial Day weekend through Labor Day weekend.

Logistics
- 1.5 miles; 3.0 miles if you extend to the School Nature Loop
- Anne Hoxsie Lane, Narragansett
- 41.437012,-71.457407
- Directions: From Route 4 South, merge onto Route 1 and travel 3.2 miles. Turn left onto Bridgetown Road at the large intersection near "the Tower." Turn right onto Route 1A and travel south about 4.5 miles. The parking area is off of Anne Hoxsie Lane, across the street from the South Pavillion. The trailhead is by the little kiosk off to the right side of the parking lot as you come in.
- www.canonchet.org

What to Bring
- basic equipment (see page 13)
- swimsuits and beach gear if you come in the summer and plan to visit Narragansett Town Beach
- cash for beach parking (seasonal; can be up to $15) and if you intend to visit the museum

On the Trail
Start your hike by the little kiosk off to the right side of the parking lot as you come in. Almost immediately upon starting your hike, you'll reach

#6 Canonchet Farm, Narragansett

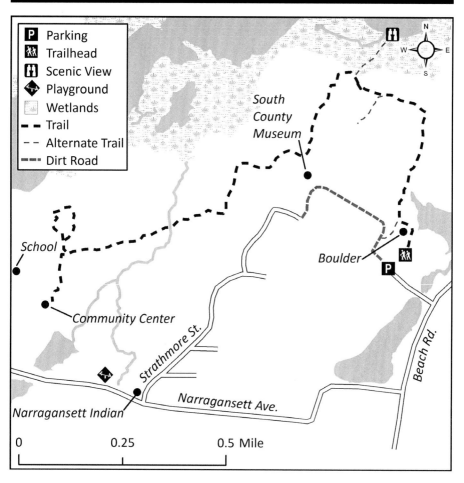

Legend:
- **P** Parking
- 🏃 Trailhead
- 🚻 Scenic View
- ◆ Playground
- Wetlands
- – – Trail
- – – Alternate Trail
- ▪▪▪ Dirt Road

South County Museum

School

Boulder

Community Center

Strathmore St.

Beach Rd.

Narragansett Ave.

Narragansett Indian

| 0 | 0.25 | 0.5 Mile |

a glacial erratic, a large boulder deposited here by glaciers thousands of years ago. Just beyond it is a view of Little Neck Pond. A little further along the trail are stone walls, evidence of the area's past use as farmland, and a beautiful view of Pettaquamscutt Cove. Less than a half mile from the cove, you'll reach the South County Museum, open to the general public for a small fee from the first weekend in May through September (check ahead for days and hours). If you wish to extend your hike, continue on the trail over a stone bridge, around the School Nature Loop and back the way you came for a total of 3.0 miles. Otherwise, take the dirt road back to the parking lot for a 1.5-mile hike.

Date _____ Time _____ to _____

Weather: ☀ ⛅ ☁ 🌧 🌨 🌬

We hiked with _____

On our hike, we saw _____

We found _____

We heard _____

We smelled _____ We felt _____

Our favorite part of the hike was _____

Our least favorite part was _____

For this hike, it was important to bring _____

What surprised us about this hike was _____

One word to describe this hike is _____

Restaurants or attractions nearby: _____

_____

We would / would not do this hike again because _____

_____

We would tell our friends that this hike _____

_____

Use the space below to draw a picture, attach a photo,
or write more about your hike.

#7 Casimir Pulaski Memorial State Park, Chepachet

Overview
This 100-acre park offers trails, picnic tables, a comfort station, and a beach at Peck Pond, which make it the perfect place for a summer hike. After this 1.3-mile hike, enjoy a yummy picnic, change into your suits, and cool off in the pond. There's even a lifeguard on duty! For cross-country skiers and snowshoers, be sure to return in the winter to take advantage of the 10 miles of groomed cross-country ski trails that lead into the adjacent George Washington Management Area.

Logistics
- 1.3 miles; up to 10.0 miles if you extend along cross-country ski trails
- 151 Pulaski Road, Chepachet
- 41.931608,-71.79674
- Directions: From Route 295, take exit 7B for Route 44 West. Follow Route 44 West for approximately 15.5 miles and turn right onto Pulaski Road. The park entrance is 0.8 miles ahead. Park at the beach.
- www.riparks.com

What to Bring
- basic equipment (see page 13)
- picnic lunch
- bug spray
- swimsuits and beach gear in the summer
- cross-country skis or snowshoes in the winter
- solid daylight fluorescent orange during the hunting season

On the Trail
From the parking lot, head directly to the beach, passing bathrooms and a pavilion and changing station on your left. Look for the trail markers on the beach just beyond a picnic shelter to the right of the lifeguard house. The trail markers are white with blue dots and lead you around the 1.3-mile loop trail through shaded woodlands. Along

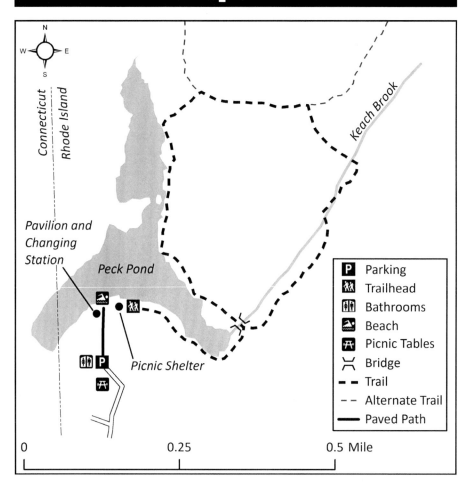

the trail, be sure to look for downed trees and stumps with the characteristic chew marks of the beavers that make their home in Peck Pond. If you are visiting in the winter and skiing or snowshoeing, you will likely venture into the George Washington Management Area, so be sure to remember that fluorescent orange requirements apply during the hunting season.

#7 Casimir Pulaski Memorial State Park, Chepachet JOURNAL

Date _____ Time _____ to _____

Weather: ☀ ⛅ ☁ 🌧 ❄ 🌬

We hiked with _____

On our hike, we saw _____

We found _____

We heard _____

We smelled _____ We felt _____

Our favorite part of the hike was _____

Our least favorite part was _____

For this hike, it was important to bring _____

What surprised us about this hike was _____

One word to describe this hike is _____

Restaurants or attractions nearby: _____

_____

We would / would not do this hike again because _____

_____

We would tell our friends that this hike _____

_____

58

Use the space below to draw a picture, attach a photo,
or write more about your hike.

Overview

The Cliff Walk path runs more than 3 miles along Newport's southeastern edge, offering gorgeous views of the ocean as well as Salve Regina University and many of the "City by the Sea" mansions. Natural and architectural beauty are pretty much everywhere you turn. In fact, the Cliff Walk is a National Recreation Trail that runs through a National Historic District. The crowds and lack of shade during the summer can hamper your enjoyment of this beautiful spot, so go in the off-season if you can.

Logistics

• 1.2 miles; 2.5 miles if you extend to Ruggles Avenue; 7.0 miles if you follow the entire path out and back
• Memorial Boulevard west of Easton's (First) Beach, Newport
• 41.485253, -71.297521
• Directions: Follow America's Cup Avenue until it turns into Memorial Boulevard. Travel for 1 mile and look for the Cliff Walk sign in the median. During the off-season, you can park for free just beyond the start of the Cliff Walk at Easton's (First) Beach. Parking fees apply during the summer season, but you can look for street parking on Memorial Boulevard and other local streets.
• www.cliffwalk.com

What to Bring

• basic equipment (see page 13)
• layers to shield against the wind
• Cliff Vanover's *Cliff Walk & Bellevue Avenue* or Ed Morris's *A Guide to Newport's Cliff Walk: Tales of Seaside Mansions & the Gilded Age Elite*

On the Trail

Starting from Memorial Boulevard, it's just about 0.6 mile to the Forty Steps, where you can head down for a front-and-center look at the surf—and maybe even get splashed a bit! To stay safe, don't climb onto the rocks from the stairs. You can turn around here, or continue another half mile or so through a stone archway, past Salve Regina University and The Breakers. At the intersection with Ruggles Avenue, turn around and make

60

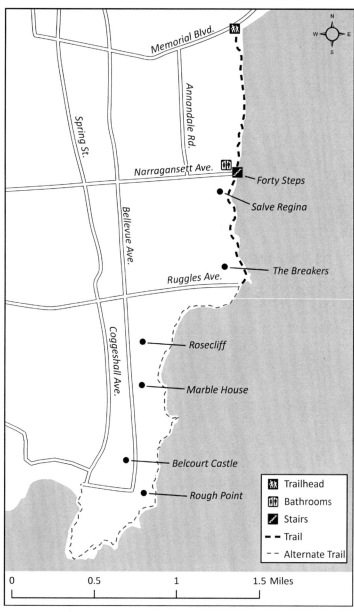

your way back for a total of about 2.5 miles. South of Ruggles Avenue, the smooth, paved path turns into a rough, rocky, and sometimes slippery trail, so pay special attention to your footing if you choose to continue. The entire Cliff Walk is 3.5 miles long; that's a full 7.0 miles if you walk out and back.

Date _____ Time _____ to _____

Weather: ☀ ⛅ ☁ 🌧 ❄ 🌬

We hiked with _____

On our hike, we saw _____

We found _____

We heard _____

We smelled _____ We felt _____

Our favorite part of the hike was _____

Our least favorite part was _____

For this hike, it was important to bring _____

What surprised us about this hike was _____

One word to describe this hike is _____

Restaurants or attractions nearby: _____

_____

We would / would not do this hike again because _____

_____

We would tell our friends that this hike _____

_____

Use the space below to draw a picture, attach a photo,
or write more about your hike.

Overview

A joint effort of the Richmond Rural Land Conservation Trust and the South Kingstown Land Trust, Crawley Preserve is a splendid property. Although a relatively short distance, the rugged paths, convoluted trails, and steady incline can be challenging for some children, and you will probably need more time than you expect to explore these parts. Although Crawley Preserve does not technically allow hunting, it does abut areas that do, so fluorescent orange requirements apply for all users during the hunting season. In addition, some visitors are on horseback, so watch where you step!

Logistics

- 2.0 miles; 3.0 miles if you follow all the trails
- Glen Rock Road, Richmond
- 41.509152,-71.60833
- Directions: From Route 2, travel west on Route 138 for 2 miles. Turn right onto Old Usquepaugh Road. Continue 0.1 mile then bear right to continue on Old Usquepaugh Road. About 100 yards past the Kenyon Grist Mill, the road will fork. Stay to the right and travel on Glen Rock Road for 0.3 mile. The parking lot will be on your left; the sign blends nicely into the surrounding foliage so the entrance can be a bit difficult to find.
- www.sklt.org

What to Bring

- basic equipment (see page 13)
- rugged hiking boots or sneakers
- bug spray
- solid daylight fluorescent orange during the hunting season

On the Trail

Three well-marked trails pass through the 99 acres of diverse hardwood forest on the property. With the map in hand, you can explore any one of them, enjoying the quiet and the change of terrain through dense

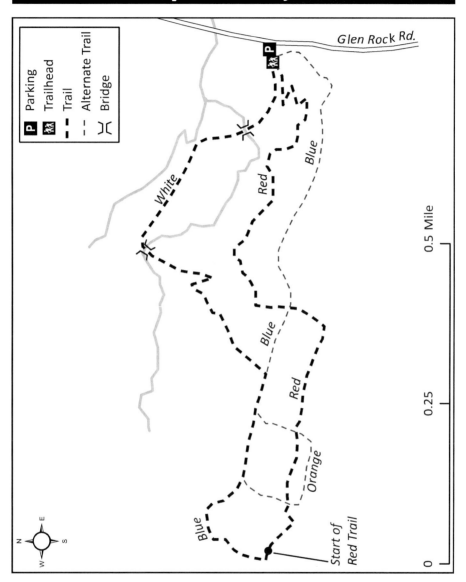

foliage and across boardwalks and small bridges. My favorite route is to take the white trail to the end and make a right on the blue trail. Follow to the end where you'll pick up the red trail which will take you all the way back to the parking lot. Take special care that you don't veer off on paths that lead to surrounding houses, and pay close attention to where the paths meet up, which can be a bit confusing.

#9 Crawley Preserve, Richmond JOURNAL

Date _____ Time _____ to _____

Weather: ☀ ⛅ ☁ 🌧 🌨 🌬

We hiked with _____

On our hike, we saw _____

We found _____

We heard _____

We smelled _____ We felt _____

Our favorite part of the hike was _____

Our least favorite part was _____

For this hike, it was important to bring _____

What surprised us about this hike was _____

One word to describe this hike is _____

Restaurants or attractions nearby: _____

_____

We would / would not do this hike again because _____

_____

We would tell our friends that this hike _____

_____

Use the space below to draw a picture, attach a photo,
or write more about your hike.

#10 Diamond Hill Park, Cumberland

Overview
Once a former ski slope, Diamond Hill offers spectacular views and a fairly gradual climb for kids of all ages to enjoy. There are various places to turn around, each affording you a beautiful vista of the valley and a feeling of having accomplished a summit, even if only a very small one! In the fall, the views are particularly spectacular. In the late spring you can find beautiful pink lady's slipper, a large orchid, dotting the hillside. The park is also a great place to picnic, and the little ones will love checking out the small pond near the old band shell.

Logistics
- 1.5 miles
- 4097 Diamond Hill Road (Route 114), Cumberland
- 42.002494,-71.419303
- Directions: From Route 295 North, take exit 11 for Route 114 North. At the end of the exit ramp, make a left and follow Route 114 North about 4 miles. The park will be on your right.
- www.cumberlandri.org/parksandrec.htm

What to Bring
- basic equipment (see page 13)
- binoculars

On the Trail
The trails at Diamond Hill are not marked, so pay extra attention along the way. To begin your hike, head across the lawn in front of the parking lot and cross a small bridge to get to the band shell. Walk along the left side of the pond, and up a paved switchback. At the end of the paved path, take a slight right to follow the dirt path uphill into the woods. There is a sign at the start of this wooded trail that says "Do Not Enter," referring to vehicles. Continue on the wooded trail that eventually comes right up against Fisher Road. Continue on the

68

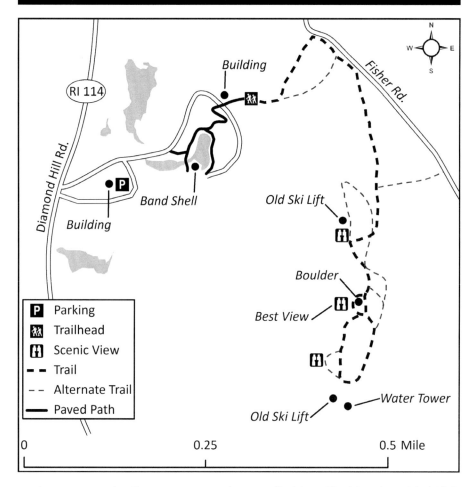

path to get to the first vantage point, easily identified by the old ski lift footings. Return the same way for about a mile roundtrip, or continue a little farther to a large boulder. Take a right turn just before the boulder up a short but steep path to what I consider the best view in the park. You'll eventually loop around, past the water tower and larger ski lift footings, and continue back down the hill.

#10 Diamond Hill Park, Cumberland JOURNAL

Date _____ Time _____ to _____

Weather: ☼ ⛅ ☁ 🌧 🌨 🌬

We hiked with _____

On our hike, we saw _____

We found _____

We heard _____

We smelled _____ We felt _____

Our favorite part of the hike was _____

Our least favorite part was _____

For this hike, it was important to bring _____

What surprised us about this hike was _____

One word to describe this hike is _____

Restaurants or attractions nearby: _____

_____

We would / would not do this hike again because _____

_____

We would tell our friends that this hike _____

_____

Use the space below to draw a picture, attach a photo,
or write more about your hike.

Overview

There are deer, turkey, dozens and dozens of bird species, as well as rare plants that make their home in and around Dundery Brook, and you'll likely see some of them on your hike. The first portion of the trail is a stroller- and wheelchair-accessible boardwalk that meanders through a forested wetland and ends at Bumble Bee Pond. In addition, there is a playground just behind the elementary school perfect for picnicking and playing.

Logistics

- 1.2 miles; 2.2 miles if you extend along the Grass Trail
- Meetinghouse Lane, Little Compton
- 41.507841, -71.175952
- Directions: From West Main Road (Route 77), go east on Meeting-house Lane toward the center of town. Travel 0.5 mile and then turn left into the parking area for the town's recreational fields and tennis courts. If you reach Wordell Lane at the sharp left curve, you've gone too far.
- www.exploreri.org/gtraillist.php

What to Bring

- basic equipment (see page 13)
- bird guide
- binoculars
- picnic lunch

On the Trail

Starting on the far edge of the tennis courts, the 0.6-mile long board-walk is easy to follow and fully accessible for wheelchairs and strollers. At the end of the boardwalk is Bumble Bee Pond. Resist the urge to immediately turn around and walk back to your car. Linger a bit on the bench and see how many bird species you can spot. And if you can, hike along the Grass Trail another half mile along the edge of the

#11 Dundery Brook Trail, Little Compton

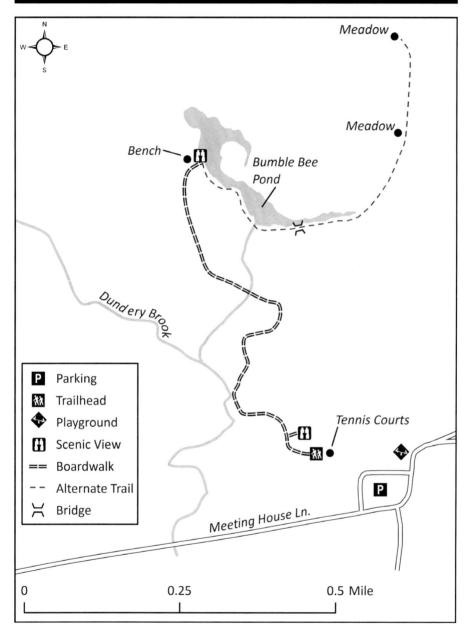

pond, past beautiful old fields and meadows—that's where you will really see the birds!

#11 Dundery Brook Trail, Little Compton JOURNAL

Date _____ Time _____ to _____

Weather: ☀ ⛅ ☁ 🌧 ❄ 🌬

We hiked with _____

On our hike, we saw _____

We found _____

We heard _____

We smelled _____ We felt _____

Our favorite part of the hike was _____

Our least favorite part was _____

For this hike, it was important to bring _____

What surprised us about this hike was _____

One word to describe this hike is _____

Restaurants or attractions nearby: _____

_____

We would / would not do this hike again because _____

_____

We would tell our friends that this hike _____

_____

Use the space below to draw a picture, attach a photo,
or write more about your hike.

Overview

The Audubon Society of Rhode Island's Emilie Ruecker Wildlife Refuge is a 50-acre preserve featuring easy and well-marked trails, beautiful views of the Sakonnet River, salt marshes, woods, a pond, and many birds, including egrets, great blue herons, and ospreys. There is also an observation blind that kids will enjoy hiding behind—if only for a short while! Though the views are spectacular any time of year, I highly suggest visiting in the cooler months; I'm not exaggerating when I say you will be eaten up by mosquitoes during the summer, and poison ivy is abundant then as well.

Logistics

- 1.5 miles
- Seapowet Avenue, Tiverton
- 41.59164,-71.19924
- Directions: From Route 195 East, take Route 24 South. Exit onto Route 77 South and follow for 2.7 miles. Turn right onto Seapowet Avenue. The refuge will be on your right.
- www.asri.org

What to Bring

- basic equipment (see page 13)
- bug spray
- long pants to protect against poison ivy
- bird guide

On the Trail

One wonderful feature of Ruecker is the map at each trail junction showing where you are. My favorite route begins at the kiosk on the yellow trail. Look for a sign for the quick out-and-back white trail on your left so that you can visit the observation blind. When you return to the yellow trail, turn left and follow to the blue trail. This is a short

#12 Emilie Ruecker Wildlife Refuge, Tiverton

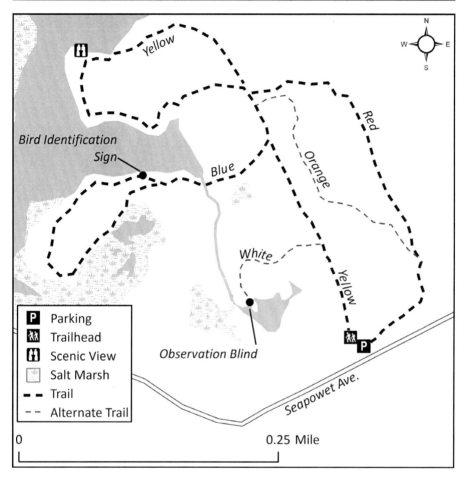

Legend:
- **P** Parking
- 🚶 Trailhead
- 🏞 Scenic View
- ▦ Salt Marsh
- – – Trail
- - - Alternate Trail

0   0.25 Mile

loop with beautiful views and an artfully designed bird identification sign. Back on the yellow trail, continue north to loop around a clearing and some more awesome views. Return to your car by following the red trail back to the parking lot. There is also an orange trail, but I don't find that nearly as interesting as the others. If you haven't had enough, hop back into your car and drive a bit further along Seapowet Avenue (less than a half mile) to the sharp left curve. Make a right onto the gravel Inlet Drive and follow to the end. There you can pick along the shore of Jack's Island, a peninsula that extends into the Sakonnet River, and find nesting osprey and literally tons of seashells.

Date _____ Time _____ to _____

Weather: ☀ ⛅ ☁ 🌧 🌨 🌬

We hiked with _____

On our hike, we saw _____

We found _____

We heard _____

We smelled _____ We felt _____

Our favorite part of the hike was _____

Our least favorite part was _____

For this hike, it was important to bring _____

What surprised us about this hike was _____

One word to describe this hike is _____

Restaurants or attractions nearby: _____

_____

We would / would not do this hike again because _____

_____

We would tell our friends that this hike _____

_____

Use the space below to draw a picture, attach a photo,
or write more about your hike.

Overview

My very first hike as a Rhode Islander was at the Audubon's Fisherville Brook Wildlife Refuge. Every time I visit I am fondly reminded of my introduction to hiking in the Ocean State—and what a great introduction it was! The refuge's 937 acres are loaded with wonderful scenery and pleasant hiking. There are bridges, a pond, a dam, a historic cemetery, a meadow, bird boxes, and more. The easy-to-follow paths and variety of trails and distances are great for kids of all ages.

Logistics

• 1.3 miles; 2.75 miles if you extend along the yellow and orange trails
• Pardon Joslin Road, Exeter
• 41.590203,-71.570436
• Directions: From Route 95, take exit 5A for Route 102 South. Continue on Route 102 South for about 5.3 miles. Turn left just before Exeter Town Hall onto Widow Sweets Road. Take the second right onto Pardon Joslin Road. The refuge is on the right side after approximately 0.7 mile. Do not attempt to access Pardon Joslin Road via Hopkins Hill Road/Sunderland Road, as a portion of this route is impassable by even the most rugged of vehicles.
• www.asri.org

What to Bring

• basic equipment (see page 13)
• field guides
• bug spray

On the Trail

From the parking lot, take the blue trail farthest to your right. In about a half mile, look for a small sign near a bench that will direct you up a small hill towards the historic cemetery in the meadow. Once you

80

#13 Fisherville Brook Wildlife Refuge, Exeter

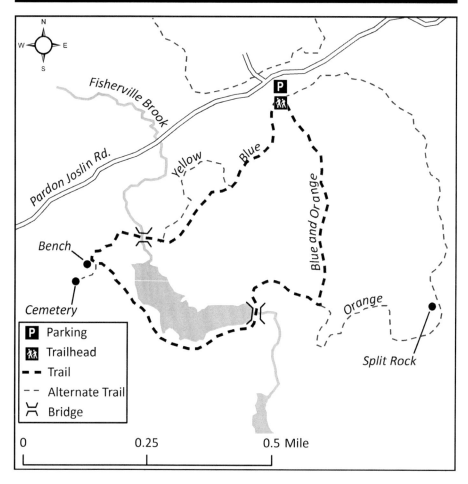

are finished exploring here, go back to the blue trail and follow to the bridge and dam (or pond overflow). You can either follow the blue loop to the parking lot or fork right onto the orange trail for a longer hike that passes the "split rock," a large rock that split in half as a result of the freezing and thawing of water within it for many years.

#13 Fisherville Brook Wildlife Refuge, Exeter JOURNAL

Date _____ Time _____ to _____

Weather: ☀ ⛅ ☁ 🌧 🌨 🌬

We hiked with _____

On our hike, we saw _____

We found _____

We heard _____

We smelled _____ We felt _____

Our favorite part of the hike was _____

Our least favorite part was _____

For this hike, it was important to bring _____

What surprised us about this hike was _____

One word to describe this hike is _____

Restaurants or attractions nearby: _____

_____

We would / would not do this hike again because _____

_____

We would tell our friends that this hike _____

_____

Use the space below to draw a picture, attach a photo,
or write more about your hike.

Overview

This 235-acre woodland was donated by the Fort family to the Audubon Society of Rhode Island and is the source of the Woonasquatucket River. With its wide, well-marked trails, beautiful ponds, diverse wildlife and a variety of deciduous and evergreen trees, Fort Nature Refuge is wonderful any time of year. I especially like it in the colder months because I find the views of the ponds are a great remedy for cabin fever. Just be prepared for icy conditions if the southern New England winter has lived up to its reputation.

Logistics

- 1.5 miles; 3.8 miles if you extend along the yellow and red trails
- 1445 Providence Pike (Route 5), North Smithfield
- 41.960846,-71.552668
- Directions: From Route 295, take exit 8B for Route 7 North. Follow Route 7 North for about 2.3 miles. Bear right onto Branch Pike/Providence Pike and travel 2.3 miles. Just after the Primrose Fire Station on your right, you will see the entrance to the refuge on your left.
- www.asri.org

What to Bring

- basic equipment (see page 13)
- binoculars to view the beaver dam across the pond

On the Trail

From the parking lot, start on the blue trail. Very soon you will reach a fork; take the branch to your right. Follow to the Pond Overlook sign and make a right. This will bring you to the first of three ponds on the property. Take some time here to enjoy the view and then continue on the blue trail for a total of 1.5 miles. For a longer hike of over 3.5 miles, include the yellow and red trails. When returning, turn right when you reach the intersection with the blue trail to compete the loop.

#14 Fort Nature Refuge, North Smithfield

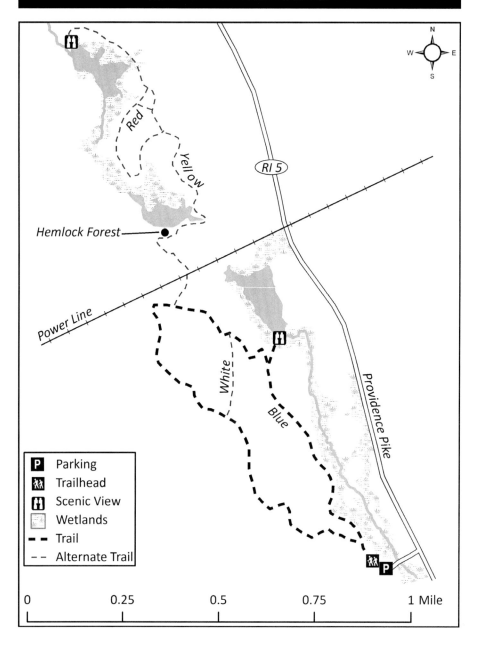

Hemlock Forest

Red

Yellow

RI 5

Power Line

White

Blue

Providence Pike

P	Parking
🚶	Trailhead
🔭	Scenic View
	Wetlands
- -	Trail
--	Alternate Trail

| 0 | 0.25 | 0.5 | 0.75 | 1 Mile |

Date _____ Time _____ to _____

Weather: ☀ ☁ ☁ ☁ ☁ ☁

We hiked with _____

On our hike, we saw _____

We found _____

We heard _____

We smelled _____ We felt _____

Our favorite part of the hike was _____

Our least favorite part was _____

For this hike, it was important to bring _____

What surprised us about this hike was _____

One word to describe this hike is _____

Restaurants or attractions nearby: _____

_____

We would / would not do this hike again because _____

_____

We would tell our friends that this hike _____

_____

Use the space below to draw a picture, attach a photo, or write more about your hike.

Overview

The Nature Conservancy's Carter Preserve boasts more than 5 miles of well-marked hiking trails through rare pitch pine and scrub oak forests and a very large, scenic grassland. As one of the largest protected areas in the state, it contributes to an 11-mile corridor of open space running from the Ninigret National Wildlife Refuge to the Carolina Management Area.

Logistics
- 1.0 mile; 1.9 miles if you include the Grassland Trail
- Old Mill Road, Charlestown
- 41.432226,-71.66854
- Directions: From Route 95, take exit 3A for Route 138 East. Bear right onto Route 112 and continue south for 4.6 miles, past Route 91, the railroad bridge, Charlestown Elementary School, and the preserve sign. Take the next right onto Old Mill Road. Go about 0.7 mile and look for the parking area on your right just before the road curves sharply to the left.
- www.nature.org

What to Bring
- basic equipment (see page 13)
- bird guide
- flower or native plants guide
- nets and containers for catching (and releasing!) small animals
- solid daylight fluorescent orange during the hunting season

On the Trail

The Narragansett Trail from the Old Mill Road entrance leads straight to the grassland. If you turn around at the edge of the grassland, it's about a mile walk. But the hike around the Grassland Trail adds only another 0.9 mile and it's definitely worth it! Here you'll find nest boxes

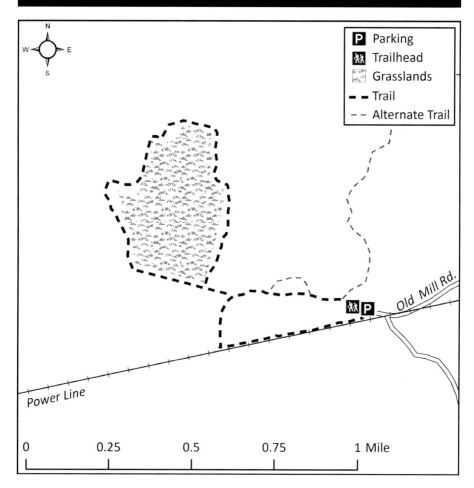

P	Parking
🏃	Trailhead
▨	Grasslands
▬ ▬	Trail
– –	Alternate Trail

Power Line

0   0.25   0.5   0.75   1 Mile

to check out and, if you visit in the late spring, plenty of beautiful flowers and interesting birds. You can go back to your vehicle the way you came in, but if you are visiting in springtime or early summer, I suggest returning via the power line, where you will encounter several vernal pools in which you can look for tadpoles and other critters.

#15 Francis C. Carter Memorial Preserve, Charlestown JOURNAL

Date _____ Time _____ to _____

Weather: ☀ ⛅ ☁ 🌧 🌨 🌬

We hiked with _____

On our hike, we saw _____

We found _____

We heard _____

We smelled _____ We felt _____

Our favorite part of the hike was _____

Our least favorite part was _____

For this hike, it was important to bring _____

What surprised us about this hike was _____

One word to describe this hike is _____

Restaurants or attractions nearby: _____

_____

We would / would not do this hike again because _____

_____

We would tell our friends that this hike _____

_____

Use the space below to draw a picture, attach a photo,
or write more about your hike.

Overview

This quiet little gem doesn't get a lot of attention, but it is quite beautiful and easy to get to. Not too far from Main Street, and abutting residential developments, there are 125 acres to explore on the grounds of the old Tillinghast factory, where cotton thread was manufactured in the 1800s. At the very beginning of this hike is Frenchtown Pond, a great fishing spot. Another noteworthy feature of Frenchtown Park is that it lies adjacent to the Frye Nature Preserve. The trails connect to give you the option of extending your hike. Just note: there are some very rocky, rugged areas that may be challenging for young or inexperienced hikers.

Logistics

- 1.2 miles; 2.1 miles if you extend along the red trail into Frye Nature Preserve
- 1127 Frenchtown Road, East Greenwich
- 41.625783,-71.505962
- Directions: From the intersection with Division Street, head south on Route 2 (South County Trail) for approximately 3 miles. Turn right on Frenchtown Road and travel about 0.7 mile. Look for the entrance on your right, just before the East Greenwich Parks building and across the street from Frenchtown Elementary School.
- www.eglandtrust.org

What to Bring

- basic equipment (see page 13)
- wildflower guide
- rugged hiking boots or sneakers

On the Trail

From the parking lot, follow the yellow Cotton Mill Trail past the pond and to your left. Be sure to continue to look for the trail markers and bear to the right at the sign. When the yellow trail ends, you can turn around for a relatively easy 1.2 mile hike, or hook up with the red trail through Frye Nature Preserve for a total of 2.1 miles. On your return, when you reach the pond but before you cross over the bridge, there is a short, steep climb

92

#16 Frenchtown Park, East Greenwich

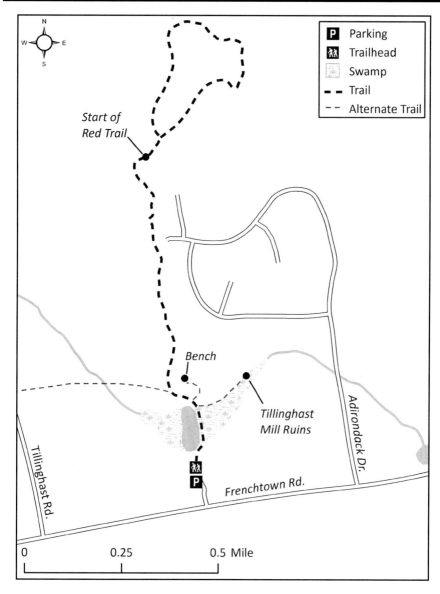

Start of Red Trail

Bench

Tillinghast Mill Ruins

Tillinghast Rd.

Frenchtown Rd.

Adirondack Dr.

P	Parking
🚶	Trailhead
	Swamp
- -	Trail
-- --	Alternate Trail

0   0.25   0.5 Mile

on your left up a sort of staircase that leads to a bench overlooking the pond—a great spot for a snack and reflection! In addition, if you would like to visit the Tillinghast Mill ruins, follow the path along the stream that starts at the break in the railing of the bridge. In about 400 feet, you'll reach the remains of old houses, bridges, and stone walls.

#16 Frenchtown Park, East Greenwich JOURNAL

Date _____ Time _____ to _____

Weather: ☀ ⛅ ☁ 🌧 🌨 🌬

We hiked with _____

On our hike, we saw _____

We found _____

We heard _____

We smelled _____ We felt _____

Our favorite part of the hike was _____

Our least favorite part was _____

For this hike, it was important to bring _____

What surprised us about this hike was _____

One word to describe this hike is _____

Restaurants or attractions nearby: _____

_____

We would / would not do this hike again because _____

_____

We would tell our friends that this hike _____

_____

94

Use the space below to draw a picture, attach a photo, or write more about your hike.

#17 George B. Parker Woodland, Coventry

Overview
Parker Woodland is an 860-acre Audubon refuge extending into Foster, with magnificent old forests, meadows, and brooks. The enticement for children and adults alike, however, is the presence of mysterious piles of delicately balanced stones, called cairns, which have been there for centuries.

Logistics
- 2.0 miles; 4.5 miles if you complete the blue loop
- 1670 Maple Valley Road, Coventry
- 41.716389,-71.698173
- Directions: From Route 95, take exit 5B to Route 102 North. Follow Route 102 North for about 9 miles. Turn right onto Maple Valley Road (across from Waterman Hill Road). Look on your left for the Parker Woodland Wildlife Refuge sign to find parking lot #1.
- www.asri.org

What to Bring
- basic equipment (see page 13)
- rugged hiking boots or sneakers

On the Trail
Start on the easy orange trail from parking lot #1 and follow to the end. Take a right onto the blue loop trail. You will go up a fairly steady incline and, as you descend the hill, look for the cairns. The tallest one has a large sign describing the theory behind these rock formations. Turn around here for a 2.0-mile hike. If you're up for a longer hike, continue all the way around the blue loop and connect back with the orange trail to return to the parking lot for a total of 4.5 miles.

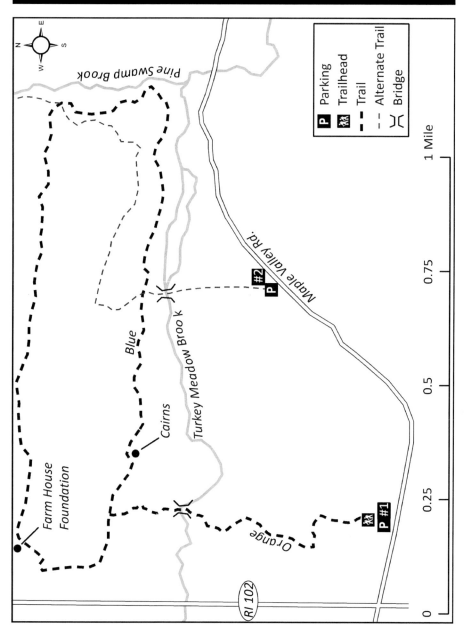

#17 George B. Parker Woodland, Coventry JOURNAL

Date _____ Time _____ to _____

Weather: ☀ ⛅ ☁ 🌧 🌨 🌬

We hiked with _____

On our hike, we saw _____

We found _____

We heard _____

We smelled _____ We felt _____

Our favorite part of the hike was _____

Our least favorite part was _____

For this hike, it was important to bring _____

What surprised us about this hike was _____

One word to describe this hike is _____

Restaurants or attractions nearby: _____

_____

We would / would not do this hike again because _____

_____

We would tell our friends that this hike _____

_____

Use the space below to draw a picture, attach a photo, or write more about your hike.

Overview

You may know of the museum, water wheels, and mills here, but tucked into the back of the 23-acre Gilbert Stuart Birthplace & Museum property is a lovely nature trail. Enjoy beautiful views of the 57-acre Carr Pond and streams, scenic overlooks of the marsh, stone walls, historic cemeteries, and the chance to catch a glimpse of wildlife, including dozens of bird species. You can also stay for a guided tour of the gristmill and birthplace, which are included in the admission fee. The grounds and museum are only open early May through mid-October and hours are variable, so be sure to check ahead for days and times.

Logistics

- 1.0 mile
- 815 Gilbert Stuart Road, Saunderstown
- 41.520106,-71.444168
- Directions: From Route 95 South, take exit 9 for Route 4 South. Route 4 merges with Route 1 South. Exit for Route 138 East toward Jamestown/Newport. Take the first exit to Route 1A South toward Narragansett. Make your third right onto Snuff Mill Road and follow signs to the Museum.
- www.gilbertstuartmuseum.com

What to Bring

- basic equipment (see page 13)
- one-dollar bill
- crayons or colored pencils
- bug spray
- cash for the admission fee

On the Trail

Before you begin, show your children a one-dollar bill. Explain that the

#18 Gilbert Stuart Birthplace & Museum, Saunderstown

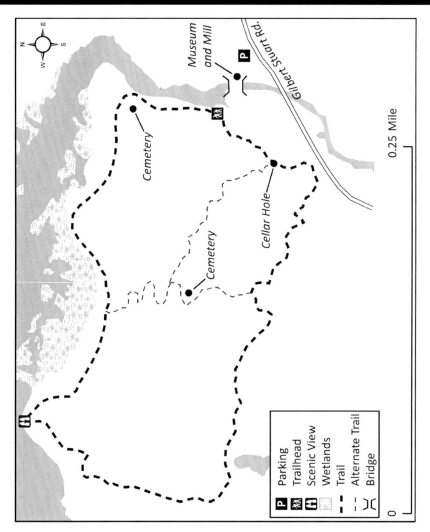

image of George Washington is from an unfinished portrait of our first president by Gilbert Stuart, an 18th-century American artist born right here on these very grounds. Start your hike at the entry gate and walk along the Outer Loop Trail. Since the entire trail system is about a mile long, you'll have plenty of time to relax on one of the benches and sketch your own portrait or nature scene, just like Stuart might have done. The trails are well marked, so no matter which path you wander on, you'll easily and quickly find your way back to the museum.

Date _____ Time _____ to _____

Weather: ☀ ⛅ ☁ 🌦 🌨 🌬

We hiked with _____

On our hike, we saw _____

We found _____

We heard _____

We smelled _____ We felt _____

Our favorite part of the hike was _____

Our least favorite part was _____

For this hike, it was important to bring _____

What surprised us about this hike was _____

One word to describe this hike is _____

Restaurants or attractions nearby: _____

_____

We would / would not do this hike again because _____

_____

We would tell our friends that this hike _____

_____

102

Use the space below to draw a picture, attach a photo,
or write more about your hike.

Overview

The 3,000+ acres of wetlands, woodlands, and meadows of the Great Swamp Management Area abut beautiful Worden Pond. Go in the early spring or fall to see the many species of migrating birds and to avoid the oppressive heat that can accompany the wide-open space. The trails at Great Swamp are quite wide and easy to walk; you're pretty much following a tire marked dirt road the entire time. However, since the path is not marked, be sure to consult the map often.

Logistics

- 4.0 miles; 6.2 miles if you extend to Worden Pond
- 277 Great Neck Road, West Kingston
- 41.469133,-71.579472
- Directions: From Route 95, take exit 3A. Follow Route 138 East approximately 9 miles. Take a sharp right onto Liberty Lane at Taylor's Fishing Area. Follow for about a mile until you must take a left onto a dirt road. Follow this dirt road another 1.4 miles past the Department of Environmental Management Fish & Wildlife Headquarters and signs for the range until you reach the parking lot.
- www.dem.ri.gov

What to Bring

- basic equipment (see page 13)
- bug spray
- binoculars
- bird guide
- solid daylight fluorescent orange during the hunting season

On the Trail

From the parking lot, you'll walk about half a mile past beautiful meadows and woodlands to a fork. In front of you, but possibly covered by brush, there is a stone marker in memory of Dr. John Mulleedy, a beloved hiking club leader. Go right at this fork and follow to the power lines where you'll bear to the right. In a short while, you'll reach another intersection. Go to your right again and you'll soon reach a large wetland, the most interesting

104

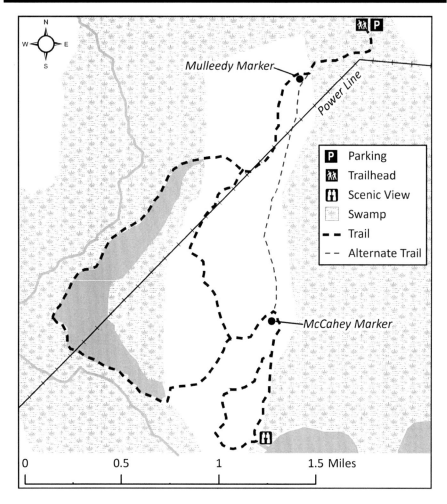

portion of this hike by far. Spend some time here checking out the numerous osprey nests and watching birds. The trail will loop around the far end of the swamp, under the power lines and up a hill as you leave the wetland area. When you come to a T-intersection, go left to follow the path back to your vehicle for a 4.0 mile hike. Alternately, you can go right at this intersection to extend your hike another 2.2 miles. Be sure to go right at another stone marker, this one honoring longtime hiker George McCahey, and you'll soon reach a scenic lookout point over Worden Pond. If you do extend your hike, pay special attention to the path you follow, as this area can be especially confusing.

#19 Great Swamp Management Area, West Kingston JOURNAL

Date _____ Time _____ to _____

Weather: ☀ ⛅ ☁ 🌧 🌨 🌬

We hiked with _____

On our hike, we saw _____

We found _____

We heard _____

We smelled _____ We felt _____

Our favorite part of the hike was _____

Our least favorite part was _____

For this hike, it was important to bring _____

What surprised us about this hike was _____

One word to describe this hike is _____

Restaurants or attractions nearby: _____

_____

We would / would not do this hike again because _____

_____

We would tell our friends that this hike _____

_____

106

#19 Great Swamp Management Area, West Kingston JOURNAL

Use the space below to draw a picture, attach a photo,
or write more about your hike.

Overview

In typical Little Rhody fashion, the highest point in our state is a mere 812 feet above sea level and access to it is a quick walk through the woods with hardly any elevation gain! Still, reaching the highest point in Rhode Island grants a certain degree of accomplishment and could be the start of your family's highpoint adventures. Believe it or not, Jerimoth Hill was once considered one of the more difficult high points in the country to reach because it was surrounded by privately owned land. Since December 2011, Jerimoth Hill has been owned by the State of Rhode Island, and access is available from 8am to 6pm daily. However, the land adjacent to the highpoint is still privately owned, so please stay on the trail and be respectful of property owners.

Logistics

- less than 0.5 mile
- Hartford Pike (Route 101), Foster
- 41.851284,-71.778969
- Directions: From the intersection with Mt. Hygeia Road, travel west on Hartford Pike (Route 101) about 1 mile. Look for a small parking area on the right (north) side of the road just past a brown Jerimoth Hill sign and guard rail. Cross to the south side of the road for the trailhead.
- www.summitpost.org

What to Bring

- basic equipment (see page 13)
- a camera to document your first highpoint
- solid daylight fluorescent orange during the hunting season

On the Trail

This is a short walk on a well-marked trail. Resist the urge to take the wider trail on your right as this is actually private property. In a short while you'll reach an open, circular, sandy area with a shed and

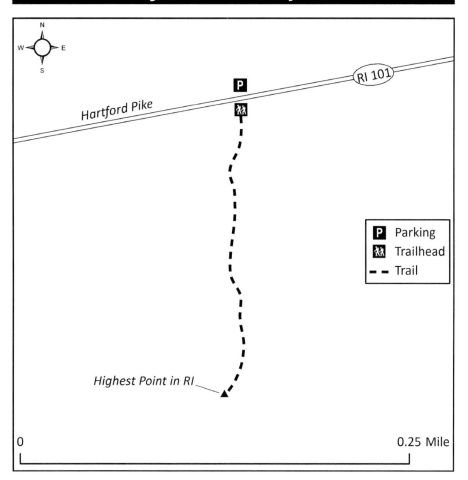

concrete pad. Just before this area, tucked off to the right side of the path, is a large rock with cairns and perhaps a little prayer flag or some other pomp and circumstance. This, my dear Rhode Islanders, is the highest point in our state! Your children will love inscribing their names and a message in the register and adding a rock to the cairns that other highpointers have started. Return the way you came, making certain you stay on the narrow path to avoid hiking on privately owned land.

Date _____ Time _____ to _____

Weather: ☀ ⛅ ☁ 🌧 🌨 🌬

We hiked with _____

On our hike, we saw _____

We found _____

We heard _____

We smelled _____ We felt _____

Our favorite part of the hike was _____

Our least favorite part was _____

For this hike, it was important to bring _____

What surprised us about this hike was _____

One word to describe this hike is _____

Restaurants or attractions nearby: _____

_____

We would / would not do this hike again because _____

_____

We would tell our friends that this hike _____

_____

Use the space below to draw a picture, attach a photo,
or write more about your hike.

Overview

Known to many simply as Rome Point, the Chafee Nature Preserve is one of the few natural spaces in Rhode Island that may be more popular in winter than any other season. The reason is that harbor seals migrate into this area in October and stay through the spring. If you pick a calm, clear day and arrive close to low tide, you're sure to catch a glimpse of these curious creatures. Just be certain to bring binoculars or, better yet, a spotting scope so you can really enjoy observing the seals.

Logistics

- 2.7 miles
- Boston Neck Road (Route 1A), North Kingstown
- 41.536736,-71.437274
- Directions: From Route 1, take the exit for Route 138 East toward Jamestown/Newport. From here, take the exit for Route 1A toward Narragansett/Wickford. At the end of the exit ramp, take a left onto Route 1A. The parking lot will be on your right about 1 mile up. If you reach Gilbert Stuart Road, you've gone too far.
- www.riparks.com; www.romepointseals.org

What to Bring

- basic equipment (see page 13)
- spotting scope or binoculars
- extra warm clothing for the windy shoreline
- hot cocoa

On the Trail

Take the path from the parking lot that leads straight towards the beach. Many people choose to continue to the end of the trail and then simply turn left and walk along the shoreline to reach Rome Point. However, I prefer to take the last path on the left before reaching the shoreline, just past (not under) the power lines. You'll enjoy a less

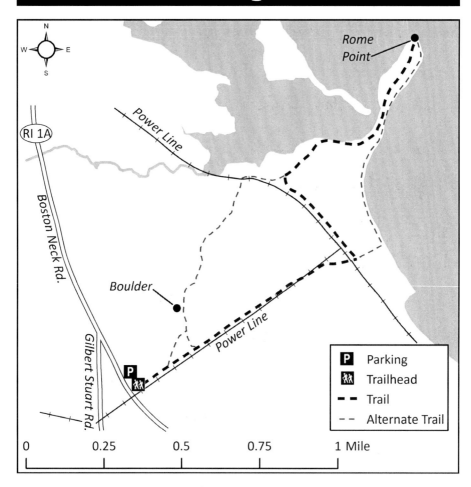

rocky and slippery route to the same seal viewing location. In about 0.2 mile, you'll reach an intersection. Turn right and follow all the way to Rome Point. You and your kids will love watching the seals, and the views of Narragansett Bay, Fox Island, and Jamestown Bridge are quite spectacular. To return to the parking lot, simply retrace your steps.

Date _Aug 25, 2021_ Time _11 am_ to _1 pm_

Weather: ☀ ⛅ ☁ 🌧 ❄ 🌫

We hiked with _the Clan_

On our hike, we saw _oyster shells_

We found _the bay_

We heard _the waves_

We smelled _yucky_ We felt _hot_

Our favorite part of the hike was _the water_

Our least favorite part was _the bugs_

For this hike, it was important to bring _bug spray_

What surprised us about this hike was _meeting friends_

One word to describe this hike is _Smelly_

Restaurants or attractions nearby: _not much_

We would / would not do this hike again because _Smell_

We would tell our friends that this hike _was short to_
the beach

Use the space below to draw a picture, attach a photo, or write more about your hike.

#22 Long Pond Woods, Hopkinton

Overview

The very rocky, steep trails at Long Pond Woods are not for the very young or inexperienced hikers. You will, at times, have to use your hands to maintain your balance, and this hike will take longer than you expect. But huge rock outcroppings, majestic hemlock trees, and spectacular views more than make up for all of the huffing and puffing you'll do along the way. The view of Long Pond is one of the most scenic in the state and was actually featured in the movie *Moonrise Kingdom*. Although no hunting is allowed on any Audubon refuge, don't be surprised if you hear gunshots during the hunting season. Hunting is allowed in the state land that abuts the refuge, but the trails do not go near these areas.

Logistics

- 2.2 miles
- Canonchet Road, Hopkinton
- 41.506223,-71.76459
- Directions: From Route 95, take exit 3B to merge onto Route 138 West/Main Street toward Hope Valley. Travel for 1.6 miles and make a right onto Spring Street to continue on Route 138 West. Continue for 2.8 miles and turn left onto Wincheck Pond Road. Take the first left onto Canonchet Road and bear left at the next two intersections to stay on Canonchet Road. The parking area, which lacked any signage last time we checked, is 1.2 miles on your right after crossing a small bridge.
- www.asri.org

What to Bring

- basic equipment (see page 13)
- extra snacks and water
- bug spray
- sun hats to enjoy the view from the top of the large rock outcrop

On the Trail

Follow the trail from the parking lot; it is marked with yellow blazes, but you will not see any until you've walked on the trail a bit. It splits almost immediately; be sure to take the branch to your right. You'll pass very large boulders, stone walls, and through a hemlock stand. After you cross over the boardwalk, you'll climb up a steep incline between two massive rock walls. You might find it helpful to walk behind your children as you are going up this steep incline, and ahead of them as

116

#22 Long Pond Woods, Hopkinton

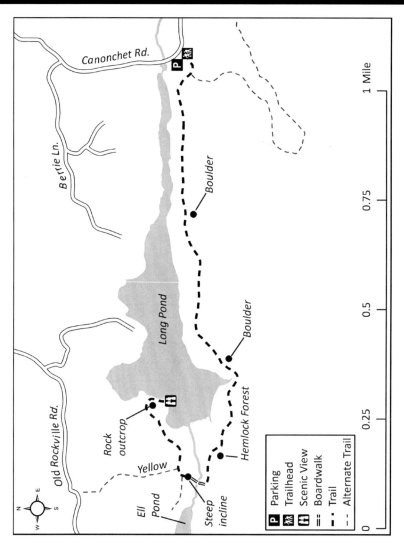

you are going down. At the top of this steep incline, you'll reach a clearing. At this point, the yellow trail continues to your left, but you'll want to take the unmarked but well-trodden path straight ahead of you all the way to a large rock outcrop that offers the most beautiful views. Take the safe route to the left (rock climbing up the sheer face is not allowed) and make your way up to the top. Make sure kids don't wander far on the rocks because it's a long, sudden drop down. Rest here as long as you can—few spots in Rhode Island are as scenic as this one—and return the same way you came.

#22 Long Pond Woods, Hopkinton JOURNAL

Date _____ Time _____ to _____

Weather: ☀ ⛅ ☁ 🌧 🌨 🌬

We hiked with _____

On our hike, we saw _____

We found _____

We heard _____

We smelled _____ We felt _____

Our favorite part of the hike was _____

Our least favorite part was _____

For this hike, it was important to bring _____

What surprised us about this hike was _____

One word to describe this hike is _____

Restaurants or attractions nearby: _____

_____

We would / would not do this hike again because _____

_____

We would tell our friends that this hike _____

_____

118

Use the space below to draw a picture, attach a photo, or write more about your hike.

#23 Maxwell Mays Wildlife Refuge, Coventry

Overview
Maxwell Mays, a folk artist best known for his paintings of historic Rhode Island, was also an environmental conservationist and philanthropist. He donated 295 acres of land to Audubon as part of his life estate and, in October 2011, it opened as the Maxwell Mays Wildlife Refuge. The trails are well marked and wind through an open meadow, forests, wetlands, streams, and an historic cemetery to the beautiful 11-acre Carr Pond.

Logistics
• 1.3 miles; about 3.0 miles if you extend your hike on the Hammitt Hill Trail
• 2082 Victory Highway, Coventry
• 41.670724,-71.695052
• Directions: From Route 95, take exit 5B for Route 102 North. Follow for about 5.5 miles. The entrance to the refuge will be on your right.
• www.asri.org

What to Bring
• basic equipment (see page 13)
• crayons or colored pencils

On the Trail
The white-blazed Carr Pond Trail is easy to follow and grants you the opportunity to see much of the features this property has to offer. Along the edge of the meadow, look for a break in the stone wall and take the trail left into the woods. You'll follow this around to the northern edge of Carr Pond. If you approach very quietly and stay a while, you might be able to catch a glimpse of a river otter or beaver, both of whom make their home in the pond. For a longer hike, follow the Hammitt Hill Trail to the top of Hammitt Hill and around the southern edge of the Pond.

#23 Maxwell Mays Wildlife Refuge, Coventry

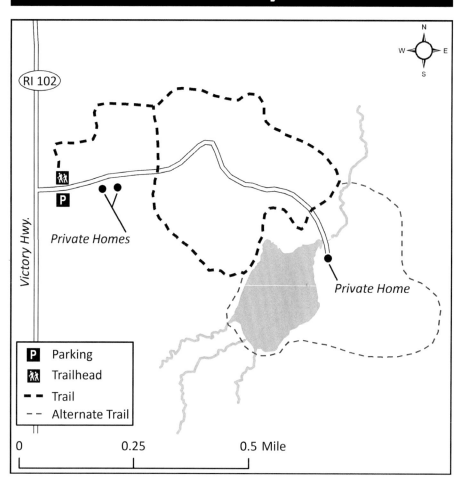

RI 102

Victory Hwy.

Private Homes

Private Home

P Parking

🚶 Trailhead

- - Trail

- - Alternate Trail

| 0 | | 0.25 | | 0.5 Mile |

#23 Maxwell Mays Wildlife Refuge, Coventry JOURNAL

Date _____ Time _____ to _____

Weather: ☀ ⛅ ☁ 🌧 🌨 🌬

We hiked with _____

On our hike, we saw _____

We found _____

We heard _____

We smelled _____ We felt _____

Our favorite part of the hike was _____

Our least favorite part was _____

For this hike, it was important to bring _____

What surprised us about this hike was _____

One word to describe this hike is _____

Restaurants or attractions nearby: _____

_____

We would / would not do this hike again because _____

_____

We would tell our friends that this hike _____

_____

Use the space below to draw a picture, attach a photo,
or write more about your hike.

Overview
The stroller- and wheelchair-friendly boardwalk at the McIntosh Wildlife Refuge is short but affords many beautiful sights and experiences in both woods and wetlands. The refuge is also home to the Audubon Society's Environmental Education Center, a state-of-the-art natural history museum and aquarium with interactive exhibits featuring local habitats and fun nature activities. The fact that you'll likely spend just as much time in the education center as out on the trails coupled with the short, mostly unshaded trail, make this a perfect winter hike. Admission fees apply for the center, but the hike is free!

Logistics
- 1.0 mile
- 1401 Hope Street (Route 114), Bristol
- 41.710694,-71.28052
- Directions: From Newport, take the Mt. Hope Bridge to Route 114 North. Travel north approximately 5 miles. The refuge is on the left, just before the Bristol/Warren town line. If you are traveling from Providence, take Route 195 East to exit 7. Go south on Route 114, through East Providence, Barrington, and Warren. The refuge is on the right, immediately after the Bristol/Warren town line.
- www.asri.org

What to Bring
- basic equipment (see page 13)
- admission fee for the Environmental Education Center

On the Trail
From the parking lot, walk around the right side of the Environmental Education Center, past the butterfly garden, and around a large meadow. On the far side of the meadow, you'll find the beginning of the boardwalk. You'll meander through fresh and saltwater marshes,

124

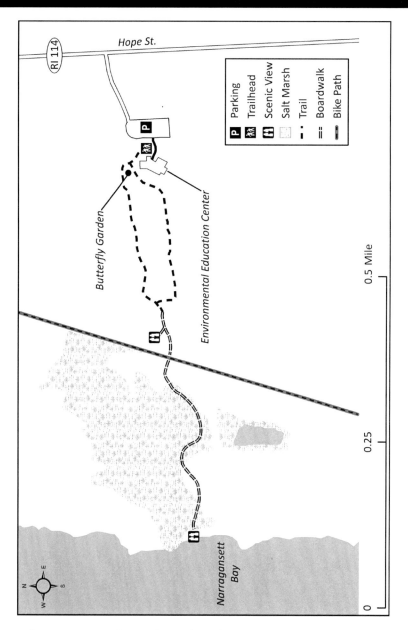

across the East Bay Bike Path, and end at an observation deck with a majestic view of Narragansett Bay.

Date _____ Time _____ to _____

Weather: ☀ ⛅ ☁ 🌧 🌨 🌬

We hiked with _____

On our hike, we saw _____

We found _____

We heard _____

We smelled _____ We felt _____

Our favorite part of the hike was _____

Our least favorite part was _____

For this hike, it was important to bring _____

What surprised us about this hike was _____

One word to describe this hike is _____

Restaurants or attractions nearby: _____

_____

We would / would not do this hike again because _____

_____

We would tell our friends that this hike _____

_____

Use the space below to draw a picture, attach a photo,
or write more about your hike.

#25 Mohegan Bluffs, New Shoreham

Overview

There are many wonderful hikes and walks on Block Island, but this one conveniently starts from the ferry landing at Old Harbor and includes a walk along the beach, a visit to the Southeast Lighthouse and Visitor Center, and a petting zoo—not to mention the spectacular views of the 150-foot bluffs. Try to visit in late spring, before the heat (and the tourists!) really hit Block Island. Call the Block Island Southeast Lighthouse Foundation at (401) 466-5009 to check hours.

Logistics

- 4.0 miles
- Spring Street, New Shoreham (Block Island)
- 41.153321,-71.555158 (entrance to Bluffs)
- Directions: Unless you're lucky enough to live or be staying on Block Island, take the ferry to Old Harbor and start your hike there.
- www.blockislandinfo.com

What to Bring

- basic equipment (see page 13)
- swimsuits and beach gear in the summer
- extra water

On the Trail

From Old Harbor, make a left on Water Street. Here you can find bathrooms, restaurants, and other conveniences. Walk past the statue of Rebecca and continue onto Pebbly Beach where you can look for shells and maybe even take a dip. Wander along the shore about 0.5 mile. When you see Spring Street directly above the beach, scramble up the rocks and take a left to continue your walk on the road. Follow Spring Street to the Southeast Lighthouse, a great spot to fly kites and have a picnic. But don't call it a day just yet—just past the lighthouse on Spring Street is the entrance to Mohegan Bluffs. A long staircase will take you down to one of the most beautiful vistas in all of Rhode Island. To return to Old Harbor, stay

128

#25 Mohegan Bluffs, New Shoreham

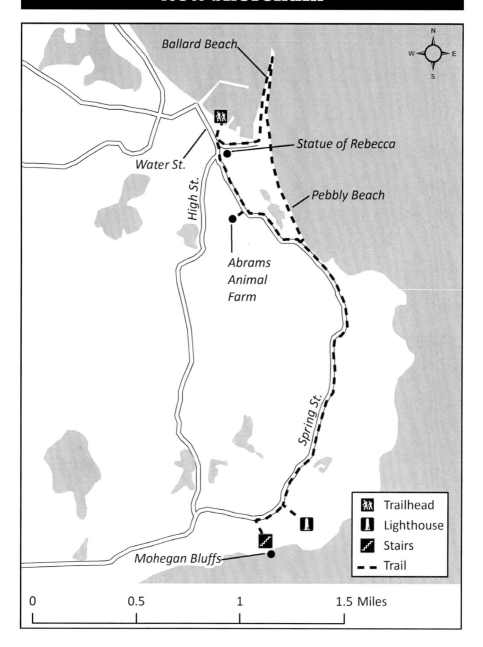

on Spring Street the entire distance and stop at Abrams Animal Farm before catching a ferry back to the mainland.

#25 Mohegan Bluffs, New Shoreham JOURNAL

Date _____ Time _____ to _____

Weather: ☀ ⛅ ☁ 🌧 🌨 🌬

We hiked with _____

On our hike, we saw _____

We found _____

We heard _____

We smelled _____ We felt _____

Our favorite part of the hike was _____

Our least favorite part was _____

For this hike, it was important to bring _____

What surprised us about this hike was _____

One word to describe this hike is _____

Restaurants or attractions nearby: _____

_____

We would / would not do this hike again because _____

_____

We would tell our friends that this hike _____

_____

Use the space below to draw a picture, attach a photo, or write more about your hike.

Overview

Ironically, the least exciting part of the Mt. Tom Trail in Arcadia Management Area is the summit, which is north of Route 165 (Ten Rod Road) and involves nearly a mile of long, straight, flat paths. But before reaching the summit, you'll experience a rigorous hike and spectacular views from the Ledges scenic overlook.

Logistics

- 1.5 miles; you can extend this hike up to 4.0 miles
- Mt. Tom Road, Exeter
- 41.564617, -71.728529
- Directions: From Route 3/Nooseneck Hill Road, turn west onto Route 165/Ten Rod Road. Travel 3.6 miles and turn left onto Mt. Tom Road. Look for a small parking area on the left, about 0.7 mile from Ten Rod Road and immediately before a narrow bridge. Be sure to cross the street and pick up the trail going northbound.
- www.riparks.com

What to Bring

- basic equipment (see page 13)
- binoculars for the view from the Ledges scenic overlook
- solid daylight fluorescent orange during the hunting season

On the Trail

This steep, rugged trail is marked with white trail blazes, which blend in easily with the lichen covered trees and weathered rocks—be sure not to go more than a few steps before finding the next marker. In addition, the rocky terrain can be slippery, especially when it's wet, so use caution along the way. After crossing the road, pick up the trail going northward. In less than a half mile, you'll reach the first and most spectacular of the vista points. Within 0.75 mile, you'll reach a makeshift fire pit and large boulders; my suggestion is to turn around here for a total of 1.5 miles. You'll have included the most scenic views and covered the most exciting parts of the trail. However, if you

132

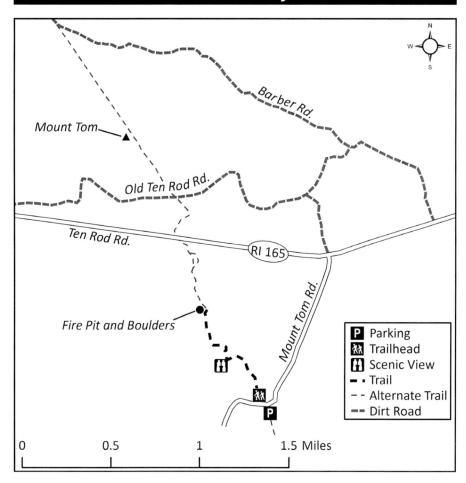

want to extend your outing, hike to Route 165 and back for a total of 2.4 miles or all the way to Barber Road and back for approximately 4 miles. Alternately, you can walk down the path that starts on the same side of the street where you parked your car. Within a few yards you'll reach a nice stream and can walk out-and-back for as long as you like.

Date _____ Time _____ to _____

Weather: ☀ ⛅ ☁ 🌧 ❄ 🌬

We hiked with _____

On our hike, we saw _____

We found _____

We heard _____

We smelled _____ We felt _____

Our favorite part of the hike was _____

Our least favorite part was _____

For this hike, it was important to bring _____

What surprised us about this hike was _____

One word to describe this hike is _____

Restaurants or attractions nearby: _____

_____

We would / would not do this hike again because _____

_____

We would tell our friends that this hike _____

_____

Use the space below to draw a picture, attach a photo,
or write more about your hike.

Overview
Visit Napatree Point just after Labor Day, when the beach crowds and tourists have departed but the water is still warm enough to enjoy. The long, sweeping views of Little Narragansett Bay and the Atlantic Ocean are beautiful, and many birds live or migrate through the area. Dogs are prohibited from 8am-6pm from May 1 through Labor Day. In addition, the Watch Hill Carousel (open seasonally, so be sure to check hours) is a great place to start or end your day. Like Block Island National Wildlife Refuge, this is truly a walk along the beach, so going barefoot will work for most of the hike.

Logistics
- 2.0 miles; 3.0 miles if you extend around the entire peninsula
- Fort Road, Westerly
- 41.310437,-71.860929
- Directions: From Route 1, turn onto Route 1A/Shore Road towards the Weekapaug Golf Club. Follow for about 5 miles and then turn left onto Watch Hill Road. Continue for about 2 miles onto Wauwinnet Avenue and Bay Street. Turn right onto Fort Road and park in the Larkin Square Shopping Center. Walk through the private parking lot, past the cabanas on your left, to the entrance at the Conservation Area sign.
- www.thewatchhillconservancy.org

What to Bring
- basic equipment (see page 13)
- sand- and water-friendly shoes or sandals
- swimsuits and beach gear in the summer
- binoculars
- bird guide

On the Trail
Once you're on the beach, turn left just before the second sign and climb over a small rise to get to the ocean side. In about a mile, you will reach an area with large rocks sticking out of the sand and water. Look on your right for a steep, sandy "path" that will bring you to the remains of Fort

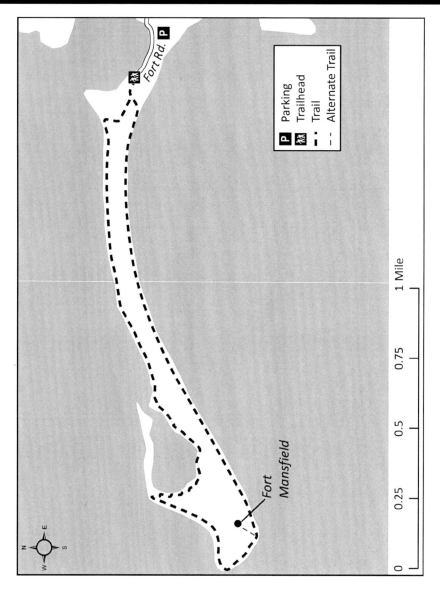

Mansfield. Climb back down from the fort and either return the way you came, or continue along the tip of Napatree Point. Once you're on the bay side, be sure to go right at the lagoon to stay to the inside of the cove along the grass line. If not, you'll reach an area that is only crossable at low tide, and even then you'll likely be in knee deep—or more!

Date _____ Time _____ to _____

Weather: ☀ ⛅ ☁ 🌧 🌨 🌬

We hiked with _____

On our hike, we saw _____

We found _____

We heard _____

We smelled _____ We felt _____

Our favorite part of the hike was _____

Our least favorite part was _____

For this hike, it was important to bring _____

What surprised us about this hike was _____

One word to describe this hike is _____

Restaurants or attractions nearby: _____

_____

We would / would not do this hike again because _____

_____

We would tell our friends that this hike _____

_____

Use the space below to draw a picture, attach a photo,
or write more about your hike.

Overview

With 88 acres and rising to almost 300 feet above sea level, Neutaconkanut (nu-ta-kon-ka-nut) Hill is the largest expanse of natural woodland in Providence and contains the city's highest point. That's right: Several miles of well-maintained trails through beautiful forests and fields, with spectacular views of the city and a significant portion of the state, right smack in the middle of the most densely populated area of Providence. With steep ascents and descents over rugged terrain, it won't take long to forget you're in our largest city! This area was the northwest boundary in the land agreement between Roger Williams and the Narragansett Sachems and, in my opinion, is the best-kept secret of Providence. The Neutaconkanut Hill Conservancy hosts various family events throughout the year, and there is a skate park, playground, and fields to enjoy—all accessible via the RIPTA bus line!

Logistics

- 1.5 miles; 2.0 miles if you extend on the blue trail
- 675 Plainfield Street, Providence
- 41.811323, -71.462041
- Directions: From Route 295, take exit 4 for Route 14/Plainfield Pike. Keep right at the fork, following signs for Route 14 East. Follow for about 3 miles; the park will be on your left.
- www.nhill.org

What to Bring

- basic equipment (see page 13)
- long pants to protect against ticks and poison ivy
- kite, Frisbee, and/or skateboard to enjoy in the recreation area after hiking

On the Trail

You're definitely going to want to refer to the map early and often on The Hill, as the signage and trail markers can be a bit confusing. Start on the red Pond Trail behind the pool. Go left to continue on this trail, which soon thereafter puts you on a steep climb up a series of stone steps known as the Great Stairs. At the top, go left at the fork on the blue Dropoff Trail and left again when you reach the orange Pinnacle Trail. Look for a short trail on your left after

#28 Neutaconkanut Hill, Providence

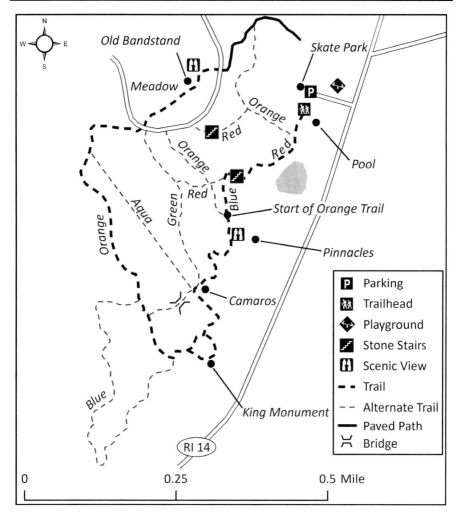

the Vista sign that will lead you to a great lookout point called The Pinnacles, named not because this is the highest point, but because the large rocks here had tremendous spiritual significance to the Native Americans. Continue on the Pinnacle Trail, past the Camaros (yes, actual cars) abandoned here decades ago when the park was not as well cared for, and go left onto the Monument Loop Trail. At the end you'll hook back up with the orange trail, which leads to the Meadow and the remains of an old bandstand. Here you'll enjoy a well-deserved rest and the most spectacular views of the city. Continue straight down to a paved path and stairs, past the old ski lift footings, and return to the parking lot and recreation area.

#28 Neutaconkanut Hill, Providence JOURNAL

Date _____ Time _____ to _____

Weather: ☀ ⛅ ☁ 🌧 🌨 🌬

We hiked with _____

On our hike, we saw _____

We found _____

We heard _____

We smelled _____ We felt _____

Our favorite part of the hike was _____

Our least favorite part was _____

For this hike, it was important to bring _____

What surprised us about this hike was _____

One word to describe this hike is _____

Restaurants or attractions nearby: _____

_____

We would / would not do this hike again because _____

_____

We would tell our friends that this hike _____

_____

Use the space below to draw a picture, attach a photo, or write more about your hike.

Overview

The trails in the northern section of the Ninigret National Wildlife Refuge are flat and easy to navigate through beautiful pine and oak trees, blueberry shrubs, and ferns. You can look for critters in a small vernal pond, take in beautiful ocean views from an observational platform, and explore interactive exhibits, displays, and activities at the Kettle Pond Visitor Center. The center is open daily from 10am-4pm and it's free! Pets are not allowed on Rhode Island national wildlife refuges, except in this section of Ninigret—please keep dogs leashed at all times and clean up after them.

Logistics

- 0.8 mile; 1.75 miles if you extend on the Ocean View Trail
- 50 Bend Road, Charlestown
- 41.367304, -71.685167
- Directions: When traveling on Route 1 South, pass the Ninigret National Wildlife Refuge entrance and travel 0.5 mile. Turn right onto Bend Road. When traveling on Route 1 North, travel just past the sign for Burlingame. Make a U-turn onto Route 1 South. Travel 0.5 mile. Take a right on Bend Road.
- www.fws.gov

What to Bring

- basic equipment (see page 13)
- magnifying glasses and boots for exploring the pond's edge

On the Trail

From the back corner of the parking lot, start along the Watchaug Pond Trail and turn left onto the Toupoysett (too-poy-sett) Pond Trail loop. Take some time to look for critters in the peaceful vernal pond, a temporary body of water that is the habitat for various species of developing amphibians and insects. When you go back to the Watchaug Pond Trail, turn right to return to the parking lot. If you

144

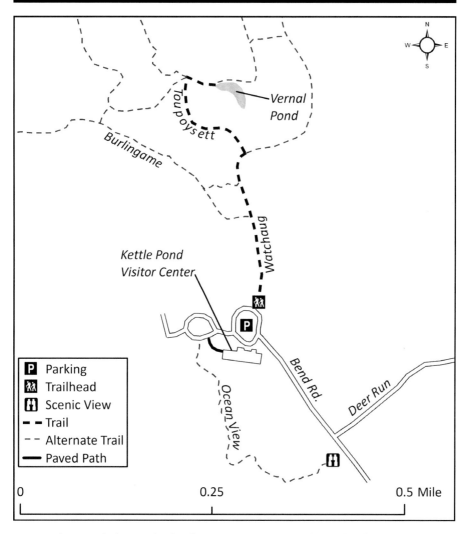

Legend

- **P** Parking
- **Trailhead**
- **Scenic View**
- **- -** Trail
- **- -** Alternate Trail
- **——** Paved Path

Vernal Pond

Toupoysett

Burlingame

Kettle Pond Visitor Center

Watchaug

Ocean View

Bend Rd.

Deer Run

| 0 | 0.25 | 0.5 Mile |

want a longer hike, include the Ocean View Trail on the far side of the Visitor Center. This will lead you to a view of Ninigret Pond and Block Island from atop an observational platform.

Date _____ Time _____ to _____

Weather: ☀ ⛅ ☁ 🌧 🌨 🌬

We hiked with _____

On our hike, we saw _____

We found _____

We heard _____

We smelled _____ We felt _____

Our favorite part of the hike was _____

Our least favorite part was _____

For this hike, it was important to bring _____

What surprised us about this hike was _____

One word to describe this hike is _____

Restaurants or attractions nearby: _____

_____

We would / would not do this hike again because _____

_____

We would tell our friends that this hike _____

_____

146

Use the space below to draw a picture, attach a photo,
or write more about your hike.

Overview

By far, my favorite hike in the southern section of the Ninigret Wildlife Refuge is the Grassy Point Trail. Kids will be fascinated that this was the Charlestown Naval Auxiliary Landing Field or "Charlietown" during World War II, but you can also enjoy a lovely hike to scenic Grassy Point. Kayaking, canoeing, and fishing are all permitted on Ninigret Pond, the largest coastal salt pond in the state. This section of Ninigret also includes a playground and, tucked behind it, a pond with a lifeguard during the summer months!

Logistics

- 1.3 miles; 4.2 miles if you extend along the Cross Refuge and Foster Cove Loop trails
- Park Lane, Charlestown
- 41.365170, -71.656775
- Directions: From Route 2 in Charlestown, travel south on Route 1 towards Westerly for 0.7 mile. Make a U-turn onto Route 1 North. Immediately move into your right lane and exit onto Old Post Road. Stay straight for about a mile and turn left into Ninigret Park, across from the Ambulance-Rescue Service. Pass the Frosty Drew Nature Center & Observatory and continue straight when the road curves sharply to the left. You will pass a dog park on your right and end at the parking lot.
- www.fws.gov

What to Bring

- basic equipment (see page 13)
- canoe or kayak
- fishing equipment
- swimsuits and beach gear in the summer

On the Trail

Start your hike on the far, eastern end of the parking lot on the paved Grassy Point Trail. Within a couple of minutes, you'll be standing on the remnants of Runway 30. Take the short loop to your left, which is really

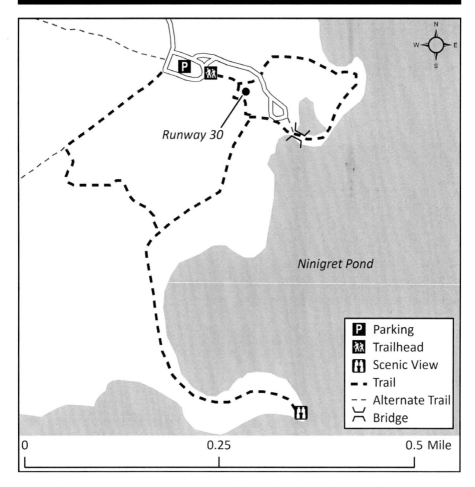

Runway 30

Ninigret Pond

P	Parking
🏃	Trailhead
🔭	Scenic View
∙ ∙	Trail
– –	Alternate Trail
⌒	Bridge

0   0.25   0.5 Mile

quite pleasant. After you cross a small boardwalk/bridge, you'll pass a gravel parking area on your right. This is a great spot to unload a kayak or canoe, as it connects back to the paved parking lot. When you return to the original path, turn left and continue straight all the way to Grassy Point. Here you'll enjoy sweeping views of Ninigret Pond with the aid of two spotting scopes. On your way back, turn left onto the more protected Cross Refuge Trail. In 0.1 mile, you will reach another intersection. Turn right to return to your vehicle. You can turn left to continue on the Cross Refuge Trail and Foster Cove Loop for a much longer walk, but Grassy Point is certainly the highlight of this hike.

Date _____ Time _____ to _____

Weather: ☀ ⛅ ☁ 🌧 🌨 🌬

We hiked with _____

On our hike, we saw _____

We found _____

We heard _____

We smelled _____ We felt _____

Our favorite part of the hike was _____

Our least favorite part was _____

For this hike, it was important to bring _____

What surprised us about this hike was _____

One word to describe this hike is _____

Restaurants or attractions nearby: _____

_____

We would / would not do this hike again because _____

_____

We would tell our friends that this hike _____

_____

Use the space below to draw a picture, attach a photo,
or write more about your hike.

Overview

The Norman Bird Sanctuary's 325 acres and more than 7 miles of hiking trails are well worth the few dollars they charge non-members for trail use. With ten different trails, there's something for everyone. Enjoy a leisurely stroll or hike the steep, rocky trail to the top of Hanging Rock. Either way, you're certain to see or hear a song from one of the many species of birds who make their home there. The Welcome Center, Museum, and grounds are open 9am-5pm every day except major holidays.

Logistics

- 3.5 miles; up to 7 miles if you extend along the other trails
- 583 Third Beach Road, Middletown
- 41.499743, -71.250900
- Directions: From the Newport Pell Bridge, follow the signs to Fall River/Cape Cod. Take a left at the end of the ramp that faces the Newport Grand Casino and proceed about 3 miles through four stop lights. (At the fourth stop light, there is a 7-Eleven.) Continue straight through the light to the four-way stop sign, and make a right onto Third Beach Road. The entrance is 0.75 mile on the right.
- www.normanbirdsanctuary.org

What to Bring

- basic equipment (see page 13)
- money for trail use fee
- binoculars
- bird guide
- bug spray

On the Trail

First, check in at the Welcome Center and pay your trail use fee. Walk behind the building to the William Holland Drury Garden where you'll pick up the Quarry Trail that travels through open fields and wood-

#31 Norman Bird Sanctuary, Middletown

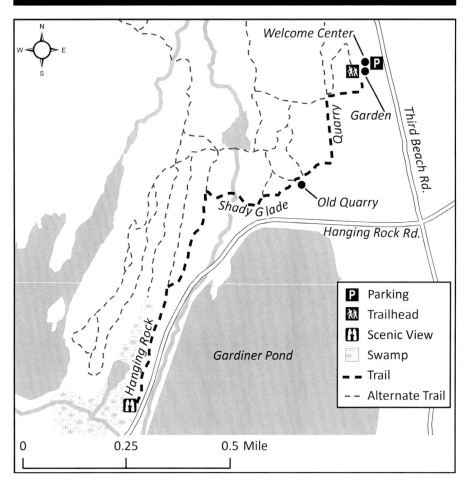

lands. Stop at the pond (which used to be a slate quarry) and enjoy the pleasant sounds of bird and frog calls, as well as the spring that feeds the pond. Follow the signs to the Shady Glade Trail and turn left onto the Hanging Rock Trail. This rocky walk along a puddingstone ridge allows excellent views of Gardiner Pond, Sachuest Bay, and St. George's School. Be sure to take extra care here and stay along the top of this narrow, rocky trail, which rises 70 feet above sea level.

#31 Norman Bird Sanctuary, Middletown JOURNAL

Date _____ Time _____ to _____

Weather: ☀ ⛅ ☁ 🌧 🌨 🌬

We hiked with _____

On our hike, we saw _____

We found _____

We heard _____

We smelled _____ We felt _____

Our favorite part of the hike was _____

Our least favorite part was _____

For this hike, it was important to bring _____

What surprised us about this hike was _____

One word to describe this hike is _____

Restaurants or attractions nearby: _____

_____

We would / would not do this hike again because _____

_____

We would tell our friends that this hike _____

_____

Use the space below to draw a picture, attach a photo, or write more about your hike.

#32 Powder Mill Ledges Wildlife Refuge, Smithfield

Overview

At the Powder Mill Ledges Wildlife Refuge, you'll find many different features along the well-managed trails, including a pond, streams, rock walls, and beautiful woodlands. Many species such as white-tailed deer, coyote, grey fox, and wild turkey make their home here, so keep a lookout for evidence of these animals. This property is also home to the Audubon Society of Rhode Island (ASRI) headquarters, where you'll find a small gift shop, library, teacher's resource center, restrooms, and bird feeding stations. Just call ahead of time to check if it is open.

Logistics
- 0.9 mile; 2.0 if you extend on the blue trail; 2.75 miles if you also include the yellow trail
- 12 Sanderson Road (Rt. 5), Smithfield
- 41.868527, -71.531045
- Directions: From Route 295, take exit 7B onto Route 44 West. At the fourth set of lights, turn left onto Route 5/Sanderson Road. The refuge will be on your left.
- www.asri.org

What to Bring
- basic equipment (see page 13)
- a little cash for the gift shop

On the Trail

The orange trail starts and ends at the informational sign next to the ASRI headquarters. Begin by going straight back behind the signage toward the meadow instead of to your right along the edge of the parking lot. Just after you pass through an opening in a stone wall, you will reach the intersection of the blue and orange trails. Take the fork to the right for the orange trail and enjoy a pleasant, short walk that includes the pond. (If you turn right before the stone wall, you'll be

156

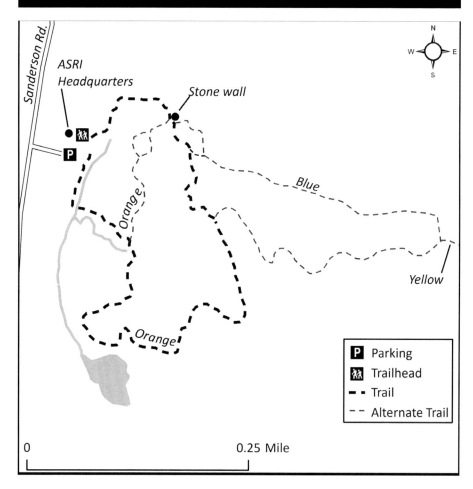

Sanderson Rd.

ASRI
Headquarters

Stone wall

N

W

E

S

P

Blue

Orange

Yellow

Orange

P Parking

🚶 Trailhead

▬ ▪ Trail

▬ ▬ Alternate Trail

0   0.25 Mile

back to the parking lot in less than a half mile and miss out on the real beauty of the property, in my opinion.) To extend your hike deeper into the forest, follow the blue trail at the first intersection instead. When the blue trail connects back to the orange trail, take a left to visit the pond before returning to the parking lot for a 2.0-mile hike. You can also include the yellow loop trail for a total of 2.75 miles.

Date _____ Time _____ to _____

Weather: ☀ ⛅ ☁ 🌧 🌨 🌬

We hiked with _____

On our hike, we saw _____

We found _____

We heard _____

We smelled _____ We felt _____

Our favorite part of the hike was _____

Our least favorite part was _____

For this hike, it was important to bring _____

What surprised us about this hike was _____

One word to describe this hike is _____

Restaurants or attractions nearby: _____

_____

We would / would not do this hike again because _____

_____

We would tell our friends that this hike _____

_____

158

Use the space below to draw a picture, attach a photo,
or write more about your hike.

Overview

Once an abandoned dump, Ryan Park may be one of Rhode Island's best kept secrets. The 350-acre park includes athletic fields, boat-ramp access to picturesque Belleville Pond (no motors allowed), a playground, picnic tables, and miles of hiking trails. The easiest trail to follow is the loop that circles the smaller portion of Belleville Pond. It has many great features including the "rainbow bridge," aptly named by little ones because of its shape. The parking lot is a bit tricky to find and the trail is unmarked, so be sure to follow the directions below. Ryan Park allows waterfowl hunting, which is exempt from fluorescent orange requirements.

Logistics

- 1.0 mile
- Oakhill Rd, North Kingstown
- 41.556766, -71.476611
- Directions: From Route 4 North, take a right turn at the second light onto Oak Hill Road. From Route 4 South, it is a left turn at the first light. Drive about 1 mile, and turn left into the second and main entrance of Ryan Park. Bear left and pass the basketball court on your right. When the road starts to curve right, take the gravel road directly in front of you to the first parking area on your right. Start your hike at the metal gate on the left.
- www.northkingstown.org

What to Bring

- basic equipment (see page 13)
- canoe or kayak
- fishing equipment

On the Trail

The trails at Ryan Park are not marked, so keep the pond to your left to stay on the intended trail. Start at the metal gate and immediately cross over a bridge. From here, you can point out the bridge that is on the far side of the pond and tell your kids that you're going to hike there. Walk past the dam and fish ladder and make sure to keep left at each trail intersection. You'll eventually come to a set of wooden stairs that leads you down to

160

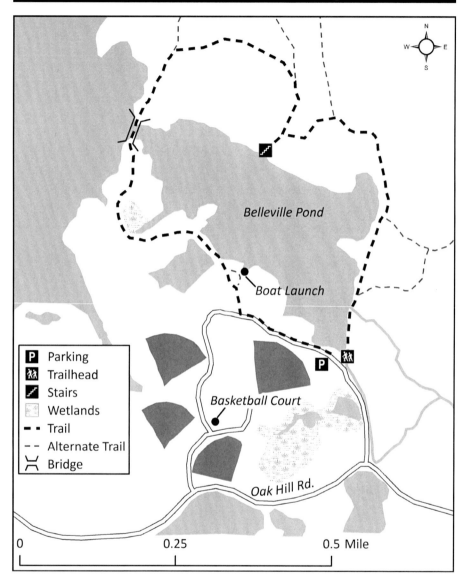

Belleville Pond

Boat Launch

Legend

- P — Parking
- 🚶 — Trailhead
- ⤢ — Stairs
- 🌿 — Wetlands
- - - — Trail
- -- -- — Alternate Trail
- ⊔ — Bridge

Basketball Court

Oak Hill Rd.

| 0 | 0.25 | 0.5 Mile |

a nice view of Belleville Pond and a great place to relax. Continue coun-
terclockwise around the pond until you reach the small arch bridge that
might have seemed quite the distance away when you pointed it out at
the beginning of the hike. Be sure to express, especially to really little ones,
how proud you are that they arrived. To end your hike, follow the narrow
wooded trail to the boat ramp and walk along the gravel road back to your
vehicle.

Date _____ Time _____ to _____

Weather: ☼ ⛅ ☁ 🌧 🌨 🌬

We hiked with _____

On our hike, we saw _____

We found _____

We heard _____

We smelled _____ We felt _____

Our favorite part of the hike was _____

Our least favorite part was _____

For this hike, it was important to bring _____

What surprised us about this hike was _____

One word to describe this hike is _____

Restaurants or attractions nearby: _____

_____

We would / would not do this hike again because _____

_____

We would tell our friends that this hike _____

_____

Use the space below to draw a picture, attach a photo,
or write more about your hike.

Overview

It's hard to believe the Sachuest Point National Wildlife Refuge was once a municipal landfill. The 40-acre refuge now includes breathtaking views, salt marshes, steep rocky shorelines, observation platforms for bird watching, stroller- and wheelchair-accessible trails, and a small visitors center, open every day from 10am-4pm. Because it sits on a small peninsula surrounded by the Atlantic Ocean, Sakonnet River, and Sachuest Bay, it can be an ideal spot for cooling off in the summer. It also attracts snowy owls and the second largest wintering population of harlequin ducks on the Atlantic coast during the colder months, not to mention more than 200 other bird species throughout the year. If you visit during the summer, give yourself enough time to navigate through beach traffic.

Logistics

- 1.2 miles; 2.5 miles if you extend along the Ocean View Loop
- 769 Sachuest Point Road, Middletown
- 41.479913, -71.243877
- Directions: From the Newport Pell Bridge, follow signs for Fall River/ Cape Cod, and merge onto Route 138 East. At the end of the ramp, turn left onto Admiral Kalbfus Road. Follow for 2.3 miles (the road will change to Miantonomi Avenue and then Green End Avenue). Turn right onto Paradise Avenue and follow 1.3 miles to end. Turn left onto Hanging Rock Road. Keep right at the fork to continue onto Sachuest Point Road, which will lead you into the Refuge.
- www.fws.gov

What to Bring

- basic equipment (see page 13)
- clothing to protect you from the sun and/or wind
- bird guide
- binoculars
- fishing equipment
- swimsuits and beach gear in the summer (Third Beach is right down the road)

164

#34 Sachuest Point National Wildlife Refuge, Middletown

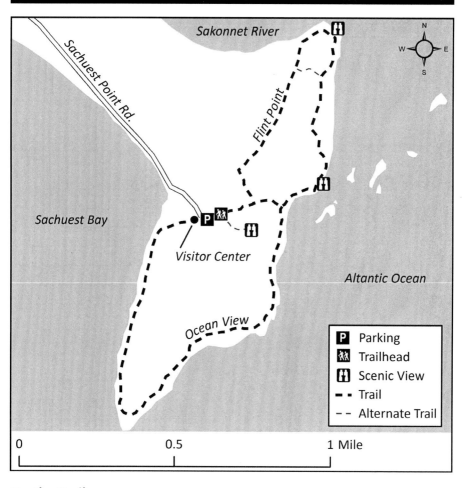

0   **0.5**   **1 Mile**

On the Trail

Both of the refuge trails start at the parking lot and are very easy to navigate. In addition, both trails offer access to the shoreline, where the kids might like to scramble on the large rocks or cast a fishing line. Hike one or both loops—you really can't go wrong!—but the shorter Flint Point Loop has a couple of observation platforms (one with spotting scopes), which I find are helpful in keeping the kids motivated and moving along. There is no tree cover on either trail, so be sure to dress appropriately to protect yourself from sun and/or wind exposure.

#34 Sachuest Point National Wildlife Refuge, Middletown JOURNAL

Date 10/15/2021   Time 9 to 1030

Weather: ☀ ⛅ ☁ 🌧 ❄ 💨

We hiked with mom, dad, Grace, Laine

On our hike, we saw birds

We found green stones & snakes

We heard birdsong

We smelled ocean   We felt warm

Our favorite part of the hike was rock jumping

Our least favorite part was none

For this hike, it was important to bring water

What surprised us about this hike was green rocks from Africa

One word to describe this hike is short

Restaurants or attractions nearby: none

_____

We would / would not do this hike again because _____

fun!

We would tell our friends that this hike _____

is good fishing spot

Use the space below to draw a picture, attach a photo,
or write more about your hike.

Overview

Depending on the season and recent rainfall accumulations, Stepstone Falls in Arcadia Management Area can be just a gentle trickle or a raging torrent. In any case, it is definitely a beautiful place to visit, and the trail along the river is quite lovely, taking you past an old quarry and over various boardwalks and bridges. You are more likely to see a good amount of water coming over the falls in the spring than in the summer or fall, but be aware that the trail can be quite muddy at this time of year.

Logistics

- 3.0 miles
- Plain Road, Exeter
- 41.598066, -71.745970
- Directions: From Route 3/Nooseneck Hill Road, turn west onto Route 165/Ten Rod Road. Travel 5.2 miles and turn right onto Escoheag Hill Road. In less than a mile, take a right at the red building onto Plain Road. Look for the small parking area about 1 mile down on your left.
- www.riparks.com

What to Bring

- basic equipment (see page 13)
- a picnic, book, or other activity to enjoy at the falls
- solid daylight fluorescent orange during the hunting season

On the Trail

Take the blue and yellow trails from the parking area. Cross over five bridges and past an old sawmill site, and in about a mile, you'll come to an intersection; stay right and follow the white and blue trails all the way to Falls River Road. Walk along the road to your left just to cross over the river, and here you'll be able to enjoy the best and closest views of the falls. Follow the yellow Tippecansett Trail on this side of the river, making certain to continue on the trail by making a

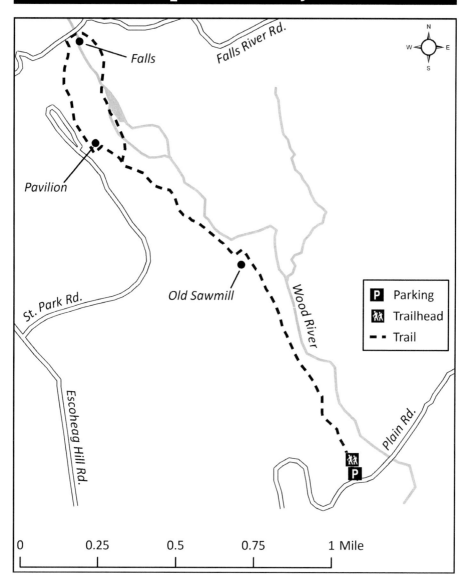

sharp (90 degree) left turn about 15 feet past an old pavilion, just after a small stream. Look for the yellow trail marker ahead of you to be sure you're still on the right trail. You'll eventually rejoin the original white/blue trail and continue all the way back to your car.

#35 Stepstone Falls, Exeter JOURNAL

Date _____ Time _____ to _____

Weather: ☀ ☁ ☁ ☁ ❄ 🌬

We hiked with _____

On our hike, we saw _____

We found _____

We heard _____

We smelled _____ We felt _____

Our favorite part of the hike was _____

Our least favorite part was _____

For this hike, it was important to bring _____

What surprised us about this hike was _____

One word to describe this hike is _____

Restaurants or attractions nearby: _____

_____

We would / would not do this hike again because _____

_____

We would tell our friends that this hike _____

_____

Use the space below to draw a picture, attach a photo,
or write more about your hike.

#36 Tillinghast Pond Management Area, West Greenwich

Overview

At nearly 2,000 acres, the Tillinghast Pond Management Area is The Nature Conservancy's largest land holding in the state. Along with Arcadia and Wickaboxet Management Areas, and the University of Rhode Island's W. Alton Jones campus, Tillinghast helps connect 40,000 acres of protected forest spanning the Rhode Island–Connecticut border. There are magnificent oak and pine woodlands, gorgeous views of Tillinghast Pond, and excellent opportunities for fishing, canoeing, and kayaking. There are also many interconnecting trails, making Tillinghast Pond a property you can revisit again and again.

Logistics

- 2.2 miles; 3.8 miles if you include the orange loop; 4.0 miles if you include the yellow loop
- Plain Road, West Greenwich
- 41.644970, -71.757026
- Directions: From Route 95, take exit 5B. Follow Route 102 North for 2.8 miles, past the West Greenwich Town Hall, and turn left onto Plain Meeting House Road. Follow for 3.9 miles past the Wickaboxet Management Area. At the next intersection, turn right onto Plain Road. The parking lot will be about a half mile up on your right.
- www.nature.org

What to Bring

- basic equipment (see page 13)
- canoe or kayak
- fishing equipment
- solid daylight fluorescent orange during the hunting season

On the Trail

From the far right side of the parking lot, follow the Tillinghast Pond Loop Trail, marked conspicuously with white trail markers. You'll hike through oak and pine woods, to an overlook on the east side of the pond and then to one of the biggest of the many glacial erratics (i.e. boulders) on

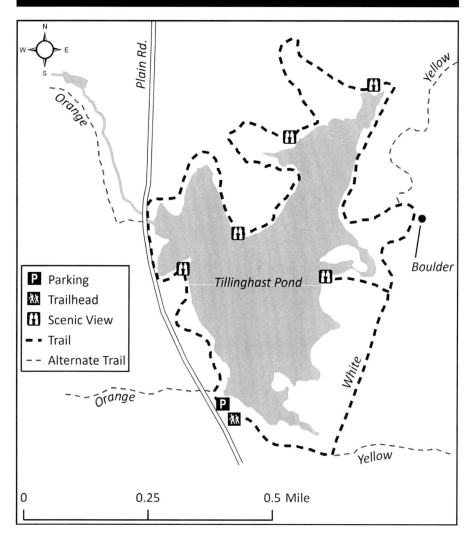

the property. Continue your hike on the white trail, stopping at excellent educational signage along the way. One of the highlights of this hike is the observational platform about halfway around the loop that allows your family to take in a different view of Tillinghast Pond. If your family is up for a longer hike, you can include the orange Coney Brook Loop or the yellow Flintlock Loop Trail. The orange trail meanders along the tops of a glacial ridge, through a forest restoration site, and over Coney Brook. The yellow trail includes a cemetery, an old farmstead, and a "boulder garden."

#36 Tillinghast Pond Management Area, West Greenwich JOURNAL

Date _____ Time _____ to _____

Weather: ☀ ⛅ ☁ 🌧 🌨 🌬

We hiked with _____

On our hike, we saw _____

We found _____

We heard _____

We smelled _____ We felt _____

Our favorite part of the hike was _____

Our least favorite part was _____

For this hike, it was important to bring _____

What surprised us about this hike was _____

One word to describe this hike is _____

Restaurants or attractions nearby: _____

_____

We would / would not do this hike again because _____

_____

We would tell our friends that this hike _____

_____

174

Use the space below to draw a picture, attach a photo,
or write more about your hike.

#37 Touisset Marsh Wildlife Refuge, Warren

Overview
At just 66 acres, Audubon's Touisset Marsh is one of the smaller wildlife refuges in the state. But the easy walk through salt marshes, hardwood forests, and meadows, and the stunning views of the Kickemuit River really make it worth the trip. Even though it's a short walk, you really feel like you are getting away from it all.

Logistics
- 1.1 miles
- Touisset Road, Warren
- 41.707790, -71.235835
- Directions: Take Route 195 East into Massachusetts. Take exit 3 for Route 6. At the end of the exit ramp, make a left onto 6 West and travel 0.2 mile. Make a left onto Maple Avenue and continue straight onto Pearse Road. At a sharp curve to your right, the road will change to Barton Avenue. In 0.6 mile, turn left onto Touisset Road. Follow it south to the second sharp left corner at the fire station. Turn right into the parking lot area.
- www.asri.org

What to Bring
- basic equipment (see page 13)
- bug spray

On the Trail
Start your walk at the northwestern corner of the parking lot. There are some signs along the way but the trails are not always well marked, so keep to the perimeter of the refuge. On this path, you'll be sure to enjoy the best views of the river.

#37 Touisset Marsh Wildlife Refuge, Warren

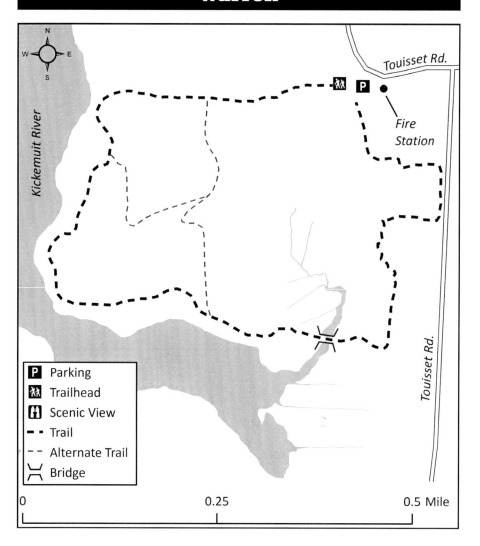

Touisset Rd.

Fire
Station

Kickemuit River

P	Parking
🏃	Trailhead
🚻	Scenic View
– –	Trail
– –	Alternate Trail
)(	Bridge

Touisset Rd.

0	0.25	0.5 Mile

#37 Touisset Marsh Wildlife Refuge, Warren JOURNAL

Date _____ Time _____ to _____

Weather: ☀ ⛅ ☁ 🌧 🌨 🌬

We hiked with _____

On our hike, we saw _____

We found _____

We heard _____

We smelled _____ We felt _____

Our favorite part of the hike was _____

Our least favorite part was _____

For this hike, it was important to bring _____

What surprised us about this hike was _____

One word to describe this hike is _____

Restaurants or attractions nearby: _____

_____

We would / would not do this hike again because _____

_____

We would tell our friends that this hike _____

_____

Use the space below to draw a picture, attach a photo,
or write more about your hike.

#38 Trustom Pond National Wildlife Refuge, South Kingstown

Overview

At this National Wildlife Refuge, you'll see a variety of habitats such as shrub-lands, woodlands, beaches, and Trustom Pond—the state's only undeveloped coastal salt pond. You're also likely to see one of hundreds of bird, mammal, reptile, and amphibian species. The hike to Osprey Point is longer than the one to Otter Point, but well worth it for a fabulous view from a large observation platform. However, the trail to Otter Point Trail is just as engaging (if not more so) and there is also a viewing scope at the end. In addition, a small "contact station" is open daily from 10am-4pm when there are volunteers available to staff it.

Logistics
- 1.8 miles; 2.5 miles if you visit Otter Point on your return
- 1040 Matunuck Schoolhouse Road, South Kingstown
- 41.383834, -71.584573
- Directions: Take Moonstone Beach Road south off of Route 1 in South Kingstown. Travel 1.1 miles and then turn right onto Matunuck Schoolhouse Road. The refuge is on your left, about 0.3 mile down.
- www.fws.gov

What to Bring
- basic equipment (see page 13)
- binoculars
- bird guide

On the Trail

Begin your hike just beyond the contact station, a great place to stop for a few minutes to find out which species have been spotted recently and to ask any questions you may have about the refuge and upcoming events. Soon you'll reach the Farm Field Loop Trail, an easy path around a meadow. Take this trail to the right and continue onto the Osprey Point Trail. Stay on this trail all the way to the observation platform. After you enjoy the peaceful surroundings and beautiful view of Trustom Pond, return the way you came. For a longer hike and the opportunity to view the pond from a different observation platform, take the Red Maple Swamp Trail to the end. Turn right and follow

#38 Trustom Pond National Wildlife Refuge, South Kingstown

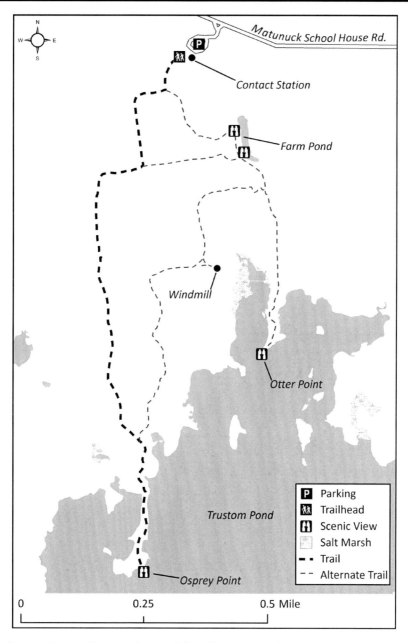

the Otter Point Trail. For a shorter hike of about 1 mile, you can simply walk directly to Otter Point and back from the contact station.

Date _____ Time _____to _____

Weather: ☀ ⛅ ☁ 🌦 🌨 🌬

We hiked with _____

On our hike, we saw _____

We found _____

We heard _____

We smelled _____ We felt _____

Our favorite part of the hike was _____

Our least favorite part was _____

For this hike, it was important to bring _____

What surprised us about this hike was _____

One word to describe this hike is _____

Restaurants or attractions nearby: _____

_____

We would / would not do this hike again because _____

_____

We would tell our friends that this hike _____

_____

182

Use the space below to draw a picture, attach a photo,
or write more about your hike.

Overview

The fifth and final Arcadia Management Area hike in this guide, Upper Roaring Brook has a long wooden walkway great for both strollers and wheelchairs. Don't let the fact that it's only 0.5 mile roundtrip throw you—you'll still feel like you're in the forest, and there are beautiful views. Plus, you have the option of extending your adventure along the other trails.

Logistics

- 0.5 mile; longer if you extend along the wooded trails
- Tefft Hill Trail and Arcadia Road, Hopkinton
- 41.560255, -71.679264
- Directions: From Route 3 South, make a right onto Route 165. Travel for 1.4 miles and make a left onto Arcadia Road. After another 1.4 miles, make a left turn just past a sign for a Pavilion on the right and immediately before the Browning Mill Pond Recreation Area sign. Travel 0.4 miles down this dirt road, passing a trailhead for Lower Roaring Brook on the left. Bear to your left when you see a gate ahead of you and end at the parking lot for Upper Roaring Brook.
- www.riparks.com

What to Bring

- basic equipment (see page 13)
- solid daylight fluorescent orange during the hunting season

On the Trail

The wheelchair- and stroller-accessible trail runs from the small parking lot to the Lower Roaring Brook trailhead you passed on the way in. It is just a quarter mile long, making your walk 0.5 mile if you only stick to the boardwalk, which may be enough for your family. Just past the first pond, however, you can pick up the yellow Arcadia Trail and blue North-South Trail. Although the wooded trails are not stroller

184

#39 Upper Roaring Brook, Hopkinton

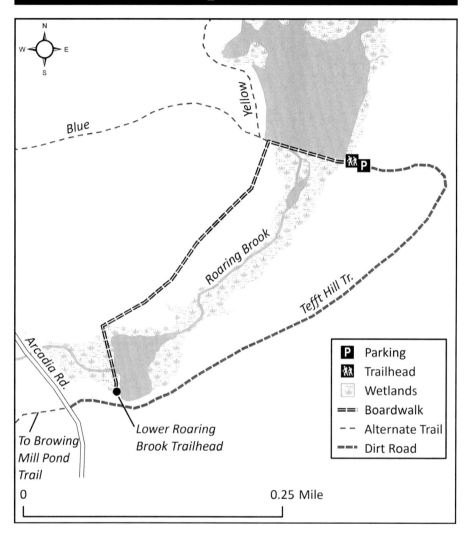

Legend:
- **P** Parking
- 🚶 Trailhead
- 🌿 Wetlands
- ==: Boardwalk
- -- Alternate Trail
- ▬▬ Dirt Road

Map labels: Yellow, Blue, Roaring Brook, Tefft Hill Tr., Arcadia Rd., To Browing Mill Pond Trail, Lower Roaring Brook Trailhead

0 ⸻ 0.25 Mile

friendly, it's worth a quick (or not so quick) "out and back" along these pleasant paths. You can also combine the boardwalk trail with the Browning Mill Pond Trail (hike #5) across the street.

#39 Upper Roaring Brook, Hopkinton JOURNAL

Date _____ Time _____ to _____

Weather: ☀ ⛅ ☁ 🌧 🌨 🌬

We hiked with _____

On our hike, we saw _____

We found _____

We heard _____

We smelled _____ We felt _____

Our favorite part of the hike was _____

Our least favorite part was _____

For this hike, it was important to bring _____

What surprised us about this hike was _____

One word to describe this hike is _____

Restaurants or attractions nearby: _____

_____

We would / would not do this hike again because _____

_____

We would tell our friends that this hike _____

_____

#39 Upper Roaring Brook, Hopkinton JOURNAL

Use the space below to draw a picture, attach a photo, or write more about your hike.

Overview

Built by Australian sailors of the HMAS Perth in 1965, the Walkabout Trail offers three loops through the George Washington State Campground and Management Area. With views of the Bowdish Reservoir and Wilbur Pond and lots of rocks to climb, the Walkabout Trail offers plenty of features to keep the kids busy. Plus, the reward of taking a swim afterwards should keep them moving along! There is a very small day use fee from the second weekend of April to the end of October, and the campground is definitely worth looking into if you have any inclination to stay overnight.

Logistics

- 2.0 miles; 6.0 miles if you extend along the red trail; 8.0 miles if you extend along the orange trail
- Putnam Pike, Glocester
- 41.921965, -71.755048
- Directions: From Route 295, take exit 7B for Route 44 West. Follow Route 44 West for approximately 14.1 miles and turn right at the sign for the George Washington State Campground and Management Area. When the campground checkpoint station is open, stop to explain that you are there to hike and pay the day use fee. Then travel 0.2 mile to the beach area on your left, near the cabin and composting toilets.
- www.riparks.com

What to Bring

- basic equipment (see page 13)
- money for day use fee
- swimsuits and beach gear in the summer
- solid daylight fluorescent orange during the hunting season

On the Trail

There are three branches of the Walkabout Trail—the 2.0-mile blue trail, the 6.0-mile red trail, and the 8.0-mile orange trail. They start

188

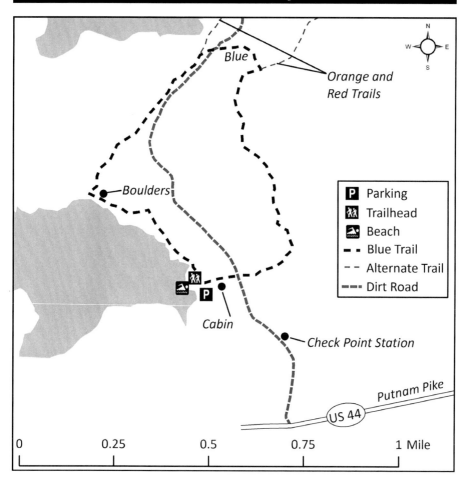

Blue

Orange and
Red Trails

Boulders

P Parking
Trailhead
Beach
Blue Trail
Alternate Trail
Dirt Road

Cabin

Check Point Station

Putnam Pike

US 44

0   0.25   0.5   0.75   1 Mile

together at the large hand-carved sign to the right of the beach.
Follow the trail markers, which are bold and plentiful, over the rocky,
rugged terrain. Even the shortest of the three trails will get your heart
rate up and take a while with little legs, so only attempt the longer
trails if you are experienced and have adequate time and provisions.
All three trails loop around, reconnect, and return to the beachfront.

Date _____ Time _____ to _____

Weather: ☀ ⛅ ☁ 🌧 🌨 🌬

We hiked with _____

On our hike, we saw _____

We found _____

We heard _____

We smelled _____ We felt _____

Our favorite part of the hike was _____

Our least favorite part was _____

For this hike, it was important to bring _____

What surprised us about this hike was _____

One word to describe this hike is _____

Restaurants or attractions nearby: _____

_____

We would / would not do this hike again because _____

_____

We would tell our friends that this hike _____

_____

Use the space below to draw a picture, attach a photo,
or write more about your hike.

Overview

With its paved path, athletic fields, and intersections with the road, characterizing this as a "hike" might be a stretch. But I just couldn't leave out this path that encircles a small peninsula, treating visitors to lovely views of Buttonwoods Cove and Greenwich Bay. There are plenty of benches to take a break and two playgrounds, one of which is nicely shaded at the beachfront at just about the mid-point. Although swimming is allowed in the park, I find that the openness of the second part of the trail makes it a bit unbearable in the summer, and I prefer to visit in the spring or fall.

Logistics

- 2.8 miles
- Asylum Road, Warwick
- 41.696501, -71.421076
- Directions: From Route 95, take exit 10 for Route 117 toward Warwick/ West Warwick. Go east on Route 117 for about 2.2 miles. Turn right onto Buttonwoods Avenue. Travel about 0.4 mile and turn left onto Asylum Road. When the road starts to curve to the right, you'll see the entrance to the park straight ahead.
- www.warwickri.gov

What to Bring

- basic equipment (see page 13)
- bicycles
- swimsuits and beach gear in the summer

On the Trail

The path is both easy to follow and paved the entire distance, so wheelchairs, strollers, and bicycles are quite welcome here! Pick up the path on the same side of the road as the parking lot. You'll wind through woodlands and along Brush Neck Cove to your left. After you've traveled about 1.25 miles, you'll reach a road and see the beachfront and playground on your left. Allow extra time to enjoy

192

#41 Warwick City Park, Warwick

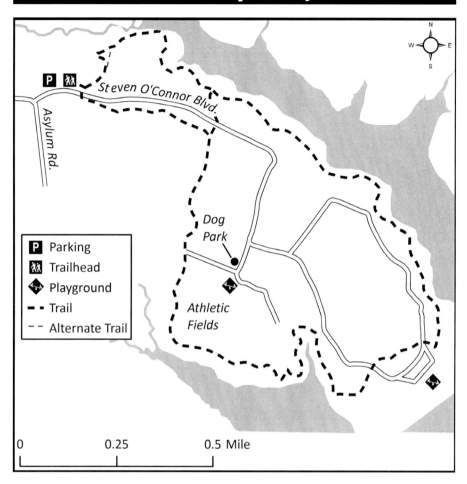

these features, especially the view of Buttonwoods Cove and Greenwich Bay beyond it. Continue along the path, past the athletic fields and the dog park, until you return to where you started.

Date _____ Time _____ to _____

Weather: ☀ ⛅ ☁ 🌧 🌨 🌬

We hiked with _____

On our hike, we saw _____

We found _____

We heard _____

We smelled _____ We felt _____

Our favorite part of the hike was _____

Our least favorite part was _____

For this hike, it was important to bring _____

What surprised us about this hike was _____

One word to describe this hike is _____

Restaurants or attractions nearby: _____

_____

We would / would not do this hike again because _____

_____

We would tell our friends that this hike _____

_____

Use the space below to draw a picture, attach a photo,
or write more about your hike.

Overview

The northern section of the West Warwick Riverwalk is short, flat, and quite pleasant. The tree-lined dirt path leads to Royal Mills Dam Overlook. Built in 1890, the original Royal Mills was one of the world's busiest water-powered cotton mills. Just look out for the poison ivy that lines much of the path on your way there—this is the main reason I suggest you visit in winter or early spring.

Logistics

- 1.0 mile
- Factory Street, West Warwick
- 41.706933, -71.519491
- Directions: From Route 95, take exit 10 for Route 117 West toward West Warwick. Go for 2.5 miles. Turn right onto New London Avenue then take a slight left onto Earl Street. In about 0.5 mile, turn left onto Factory Street. Park at the West Warwick Community Center, about 0.2 mile up on your right.
- www.westwarwickri.org

What to Bring

- basic equipment (see page 13)
- long pants and socks to protect against poison ivy

On the Trail

The path begins at the Community Center parking lot and follows along the south branch of the Pawtuxet River. You'll reach the Royal Mills Dam Overlook in 0.5 mile. Rest and enjoy this spot before turning around and returning on the same path.

#42 West Warwick Riverwalk, West Warwick

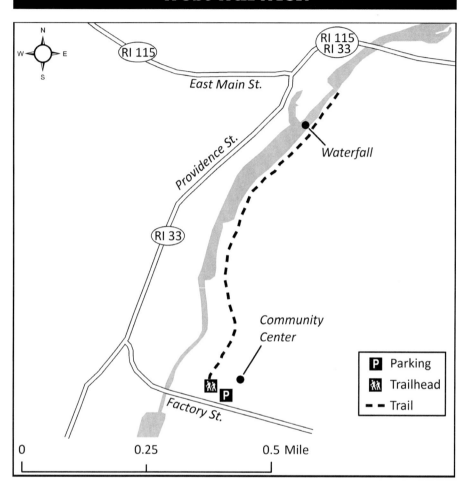

N
W E
S

RI 115

RI 115
RI 33

East Main St.

Providence St.

Waterfall

RI 33

Community
Center

P Parking
Trailhead
- - Trail

Factory St.

0   0.25   0.5 Mile

Date _____ Time _____ to _____

Weather: ☀ ⛅ ☁ 🌧 🌨 🌬

We hiked with _____

On our hike, we saw _____

We found _____

We heard _____

We smelled _____ We felt _____

Our favorite part of the hike was _____

Our least favorite part was _____

For this hike, it was important to bring _____

What surprised us about this hike was _____

One word to describe this hike is _____

Restaurants or attractions nearby: _____

_____

We would / would not do this hike again because _____

_____

We would tell our friends that this hike _____

_____

Use the space below to draw a picture, attach a photo,
or write more about your hike.

Appendix: Research on the Effects of Spending Time in Nature

Many of the sources below are compiled in:

Children and Nature Network. (2012). Health Benefits to Children from Contact with the Outdoors & Nature. Minneapolis, MN: Charles, C. & Senauer Loge, A.

National Environmental Education Foundation. (2011). Fact Sheet: Children's Health and Nature. Retrieved from http://www.neefusa.org/assets/files/NIFactSheet.pdf.

Sources

Association of Fish & Wildlife Agencies. (2010). Benefits of outdoor skills to health, learning and lifestyle: A literature review. Fort Collins, CO: Cottrell, S., & Raadik-Cottrell, J.

Bell, J. F., Wilson, J. S., & Liu, G. C. (2008). Neighborhood greenness and 2-Year changes in body mass index of children and youth. American Journal of Preventive Medicine, 35(6), 547–553.

Burdette, H., & Whitaker, R. (2005). Resurrecting free play in young children: Looking beyond fitness and fatness to attention, affiliation, and affect. Archives of Pediatrics and Adolescent Medicine, 159(1), 46–50.

Cleland, V., Crawford, D., Baur, L. A., Hume, C., Timperio, A., & Salmon, J. (2008). A prospective examination of children's time spent outdoors, objectively measured physical activity and overweight. International Journal of Obesity, 32(11), 1685–1693.

Council on Sports Medicine and Fitness and Council on School Health. (2006). Active healthy living: Prevention of childhood obesity through increased physical activity. Pediatrics, 117(5), 1834–1842.

Fjortoft, I. (2004). Landscape as playscape: The effects of natural environments on children's play and motor development. Children, Youth and Environments, 14(2), 21–44.

Ginsburg, K.R., American Academy of Pediatrics Committee on Communications, & American Academy of Pediatrics Committee on Psychosocial Aspects of Child and Family Health. (2007). The importance of play in promoting healthy child development and maintaining strong parent-child bonds. Pediatrics, 119(1), 182–191.

Greenspace Scotland. (2008). Greenspace and quality of life: A critical literature review. Stirling, UK: Bell, S., Hamilton, V., Montarzino, A., Rothnie, H., Travlou, P., & Alves, S.

Kellert, S. R. (2005). Building for life: Designing and understanding the human-nature connection. Washington, DC: Island Press.

Kimbro, R. T., Brooks-Gunn, J., & McLanahan, S. (2011). Young children in urban areas: Links among neighborhood characteristics, weight status, outdoor play, and television watching. Social Science & Medicine, 72(5), 668–676.

Larson, L. R., Castleberry, S. B., & Green, G. T. (2010). Effects of an environmental education program on the environmental orientations of children from different gender, age, and ethnic groups. Journal of Park and Recreation Administration, 28(3), 95–113.

Little, H., & Wyver, S. (2008). Outdoor play: Does avoiding the risks reduce the benefits? Australian Journal of Early Childhood, 33(2), 33–40.

Maas, J., Verheij, R.A., de Vries, S., Spreeuwenberg, P., Schellevis, F. G., Groenewegen, P. P. (2009). Morbidity is related to a green living environment. Journal of Epidemiology and Community Health, 63(12), 967–973.

McCurdy, L. E., Winterbottom, K. E., Mehta, S. S., & Roberts, J. R. (2010). Using nature and outdoor activity to improve children's health. Current Problems in Pediatric and Adolescent Health Care, 40(5), 102–117.

Ozdemir, A., & Yilmaz, O. (2008). Assessment of outdoor school environments and physical activity in Ankara's primary schools. Journal of Environmental Psychology, 28(3), 287–300.

Rahman, T., Cushing, R., & Jackson, R. J. (2011). Contributions of built environment to childhood obesity. Mount Sinai Journal of Medicine: A Journal of Translational and Personalized Medicine, 78(1), 49–57.

Ridgers, N. D., & Sayers, J. (2010). Natural play in the forest: A pilot evaluation of a forest school [Powerpoint presentation]. Retrieved from http://www.forestry.gov.uk/pdf/trees_and_society_Apr2010_Sayers.pdf/$file/trees_and_society_Apr2010_Sayers.pdf

Robert Wood Johnson Foundation. (2010). The state of play: Gallup survey of principals on school recess. Retrieved from http://www.rwjf.org/content/dam/web-assets/2010/02/the-state-of-play.

Rose, K. A., Morgan, I. G., Ip, J., Kifley, A., Huynh, S., Smith, W., & Mitchell, P. (2008). Outdoor activity reduces the prevalence of myopia in children. Ophthalmology, 115(8), 1279–1285.

Taylor, A. F., Kuo, F. E., & Sullivan, W.C. (2001). Coping with ADD: The surprising connection to green play settings. Environment and Behavior, 33(1), 54–77.

Taylor, A.F., Kuo, F.E. & Sullivan, W.C. (2002). Views of nature and self-discipline: Evidence from inner city children. Journal of Environmental Psychology, 22, 49–63.

Taylor, A. F., & Kuo, F. E. (2004). A potential natural treatment for attention-deficit/hyperactivity disorder: Evidence from a national study. The American Journal of Public Health, 94(9), 1580–1586.

Taylor, A. F., & Kuo, F. E. (2008). Children with attention deficits concentrate better after walk in the park. Journal of Attention Disorders, 12(5), 402–409.

Taylor, A. F., & Kuo, F. (2011). Could exposure to everyday green spaces help treat ADHD? Evidence from children's play settings. Applied Psychology: Health and Well-Being, 3(3), 281–303.

The Trust for Public Land. (2006). The benefits of parks: Why America needs more city parks and open space. San Francisco, CA: Sherer, P. M.

Thompson Coon, J., Boddy, K., Stein, K., Whear, R., Barton, J., & Depledge, M. H. (2011). Does participating in physical activity in outdoor natural environments have a greater effect on physical and mental wellbeing than physical activity indoors? A systematic review. Environmental Science & Technology, 45(5), 1761–1772.

Trent-Brown, S. A., Vanderveen, J. D., Cotter, R., Hawkins, K., Schab, A., Dykstra, S., & Frisella, A. (2011). Effects of a nature-based science enrichment program on preschool children's health, activity preferences, self-efficacy, and cognition. Holland, MI: Outdoor Discovery Center Macatawa Greenway.

University of Essex Department of Biological Sciences. (2011). The health benefits of the Youth Outdoor Experience (YOE) project: A short report for Natural England and Suffolk Wildlife Trust. Colchester, UK: Wood, C., Hine, R., & Barton, J.

van den Berg, A. E., & van den Berg, C. G. (2011). A comparison of children with ADHD in a natural and built setting. Child: Care, Health, and Development,

37(3), 430–439

Wells, N. M. (2000). At home with nature: Effects of 'greenness' on children's cognitive functioning. Environment and Behavior, 32(6), 775–795.
Wells, N. M., & Evans, G. W. (2003). Nearby nature: A buffer of life stress among rural children. Environment and Behavior, 35(3), 311–330.

Wolch, J., Jerrett, M., Reynolds, K., McConnell, R., Chang, R., Dahmann, N., . . . Berhane, K. (2010). Childhood obesity and proximity to urban parks and recreational resources: A longitudinal cohort study. Health & Place, 17(1), 207–214.

Wright, K. P., McHill, A. W., Birks, B. R., Griffin, B. R., Rusterholz, T., & Chinoy, E. D. (2013). Entrainment of the human circadian clock to the natural light-dark cycle. Current Biology, 23(16), 1554–1558.

Yale University School of Forestry and Environmental Studies. (1998). A national study of outdoor wilderness experience. New Haven, CT: Kellert, S. R., & Derr, V.

Index

Names of hikes appear in bold.